MW00572746

Ghosts of Valley Forge and Phoenixville

D. P. Roseberry

Schiffer Publishing Ltd

4880 Lower Valley Road   Atglen, Pennsylvania   19310

Dedication

In Memory of George and J.C.
Two reasons that I need to believe in ghosts.

Published by Schiffer Publishing Ltd.
4880 Lower Valley Road
Atglen, PA 19310
Phone: (610) 593-1777; Fax: (610) 593-2002
E-mail: Info@schifferbooks.com

For the largest selection of fine reference books on this and related subjects, please visit our web site at **www. schifferbooks.com**
We are always looking for people to write books on new and related subjects. If you have an idea for a book please contact us at the above address.

This book may be purchased from the publisher.
Include $3.95 for shipping.
Please try your bookstore first.
You may write for a free catalog.

In Europe, Schiffer books are distributed by
Bushwood Books
6 Marksbury Ave.
Kew Gardens
Surrey TW9 4JF England
Phone: 44 (0) 20 8392-8585; Fax: 44 (0) 20 8392-9876
E-mail: info@bushwoodbooks.co.uk
Website: www.bushwoodbooks.co.uk
Free postage in the U.K., Europe; air mail at cost.

Other Schiffer Books by D.P. Roseberry
Greetings from Burlington, Vermont. Mary L. Martin & Dinah Roseberry.
Greetings from Cincinnati. Mary L. Martin & Dinah Roseberry.
Greetings from Houston, Texas. Mary L. Martin & Dinah Roseberry.

Other Schiffer Books on Related Subjects
Baltimore's Harbor Haunts: True Ghost Stories. Melissa Rowell & Amy Lynwander.
California Ghosts. Preston E. Dennett.
Connecticut Ghosts: Spirits in the State of Steady Habits. Elaine M. Kuzmeskus.
Creepy Colleges and Haunted Universities. Cynthia Thuma & Catherine Lower.

Designed by Mark David Bowyer
Type set in Zaph Chancery Bd BT / News Gothic BT
ISBN: 978-0-7643-2633-2
Printed in China

Contents

Acknowledgments

A special thanks to:

- The Chester County Paranormal Research Society and their dedicated members Mark Sarro, Katherine Sarro, Kim Ritchie, Cindy Starr-Witman, Carol Starr, Ruth Himes, Karen Rodemich, Michelle Rainey, Kyle Heller, and Isaac Davis, for providing guidance, photographs, training, story research, materials, and encouragement for the development of this book—and for becoming good friends along the ghostly way;
- All story contributors and businesses who worked to see that the stories of Phoenixville and Valley Forge were told;
- Kim Cooley of The Phoenixville Area Chamber of Commerce and John Kelly of the Phoenixville Library for allowing a professional investigation of their ghosts;
- The skill and professional involvement of my editor, Jeff Snyder;
- Carroll Roseberry, Barry Taglieber, and Joseph W. Stabler for my ghostly photography;
- The Colonial Theatre for supporting the gathering of stories at the BlobFest and for providing photography;
- Sheila Cain-Coghill, Andrea Martnishn, and Connie Bretz for invaluable information and insight; and
- My patient and knowledgeable editor, Jeff Snyder and Schiffer's very talented designer, Mark David Bowyer.

Trademarks Disclaimer

Foreword

I come to you with some ghost experience. Not much, when you consider the masses in the world who've had strange and terrifying occurrences that have been known to turn hair white or burn knuckle marks into armchairs—but I've gained some experience over the years. I'm not a regular hunter of creatures that go bump in the night or phantoms that leave telltale signs as they move in and out of our so-called reality. But there are enough bizarre incidents happening around me to make me a full-blown believer of the supernatural world that exists right in this very place, in the same breath, and in the same fraction of a second that we call life. We may not see it, but it's there. Yes, I believe in ghosts.

PJs and Ouijas

I first touched the ghostly world at the tender age of fifteen while at a pajama party attended by several of my closest crazy friends. Alas, most girls at fifteen participating in this kind of social gathering can be called crazy to some degree. Parties and the questionable behavior taking place at these events is a ritual—a right of passage, a girl gathering of gibberish and playful antics that seem so important at the time. Though I know that most people have a clear understanding of the nature of such a party, let me say that we were a gaggle of girls, intent on raising hell for the better part of a night into the wee morning hours—a nightmare to sane chaperoning adults. This, then, was the setting for my first ghostly "encounter."

Naturally high on caffeine soda and salty potato chips, our hostess pulled out a marvel-of-the-time toy Ouija (said wee-ga or sometimes, wee-gee) Board that was hidden deep in the back of her closet behind the winter coats and stacks of *Life* magazine. Back then, none of us had a notion that this paranormal contraption, used to tell the future, might be dangerous or, at the very least, unsettling as is taught today by some psychics and those with intuitive ability. Rather, it was a way to find out who we would marry, when our first real loves would arrive, and whether the latest teen heart-throb would find his way to Owings Mills, Maryland, (and vicinity) to sweep one of us up onto a white charger and ride into the clouds for that life of happily-ever-after. (Ah, youth.)

At first, the entertainment aspect of this "toy" was questionable. The planchette (a triangular little device held up by two casters and a vertical pointer that, when lightly touched by two sets of fingertips, spells out messages that can be seen letter by letter through a clear round opening on the top of the triangle) would not move. One by one, we switched places around the board until it found the two people who seemed most suitable for a supernatural encounter. Of course, yours truly and my close friend (whose name I shall protect, least she be reminded of this strange night and object to having her good name plastered about the world for merely being part of this supernatural experience) were the chosen ones.

As our fingers rested on the planchette, it started to spell words by moving around the lettered board—slowly at first, and then much more quickly. The spirit in the board found us appealing enough to talk in general girly gibberish for a while. It was fun.

The other girls accused us right away of deception. They believed that we were moving the planchette ourselves—pushing it with our fingertips to spell the words we wanted to see. This was a hoax, a cheap trick to make them think that the answers given by the board were real! After all, some of the predictions were less than attractive to the young ears of those listening. (No one liked the idea of growing up and having children at this stage in life. Who needed to know that kind of thing at fifteen?)

My friend and I were both angered by our friends' attack, and we responded by truthfully whining, "We're not moving it! This is real!" And it was true; we weren't moving it. It *was* real. The board had a mind of its own. (Hmmm. A board with a mind. Sounds suspicious to me even at this late date.)

But all was not to proceed in such a fun-loving fashion for very long. It was about this time that the board became...belligerent. Though I don't recall the predications, discussion, or too many of the bad words that followed to make us feel the malevolent aura that the activity had taken on, I do remember the climatic incident that convinced me that there was, indeed, a ghostly dimension beyond the one I knew.

Our stereo was booming quite loudly during this activity—the latest Beatle album (Yes, this was before CDs were thought of, and we were using record players to play vinyl albums). The group's steady beat offered a symbolic background to our laughing teenage group. It was an easy time—a time of little care—a time of boys with Beatle haircuts.

My fingers continued to rest lightly on the planchette, as did those of my friend. We'd asked a question. It wasn't an important question, as I recall. Trivial. Probably even silly. But no answer materialized on the board in front of us. The planchette sat still. We asked another question. Still nothing. The crowd around us was becoming restless and bored. (Attention spans were not lengthy at this age.)

But then the planchette began moving in small loops. Tight little circles. I could feel a rush of…something…go through my fingers. I question it even as I write about it now. Was this feeling really there? Had I imagined it?

An electric anger seemed to pulse from the planchette as it began to speed up, moving round and round in larger and larger circles. That tingly sensation moved up my fingers to my hands and arms. Gooseflesh erupted. When I looked up from the board to my friend's eyes, I found her looking at me in the same fearful wonder that I was feeling. This was bizarre.

The planchette finally began to spell. Each letter was chosen with quick jerks; and the girls around us spelled out loud as it sped across the board.

T U R N O F F T H E M U S I C

The planchette spelled; and then respelled and respelled and respelled. Faster and faster. *Turn off the music.*

One of the girls called out with a laugh in her voice, "If you don't like the music, turn it off yourself!"

When she spoke the threat, my friend and I pulled our hands back from the planchette as though burned. This was not good.

We both felt it and just sat there in silence. Waiting. No one there believed that we were really getting messages from beyond—from some place and someone not living. Not breathing. Not part of the festivities.

But we also knew that we were not moving the device ourselves. We were the only ones who positively knew this. Our eyes were big with distress, and gooseflesh remained on our arms. We knew instinctively that something was about to happen that would change our beliefs about ghosts and the world beyond life.

Suddenly the lights in the room dimmed and then brightened again. The Beatles album began to drag on the phonograph as the turntable slowed, their voices pulled out in low groaning growls of sound. Then the phonograph completely stopped, the tone arm remaining stately in the middle of the record as if it were waiting to start up again once someone brought the power back.

But the power was there. Lights blazed in the room. Only the phonograph lacked the power to continue. One girl checked the outlet. The record player was plugged in. All was as it should be—except that the music had been turned off.

Silence held the room with a frosty grip. The other girls in our group sat wide-eyed and shocked. (Maybe this wasn't a trick after all!) I got up slowly, took the tone arm off the stopped record, and turned the phonograph switch to *off*. Looking up to the group of girls, I said, "Ditch the Ouija Board." I walked from the room and as far as I know, none of us has spoken of the incident since. At least not me. Until this day.

I'm not even sure what happened to the board after that.

It was later that I found that many such incidents had taken place in this particular house. These were things that the family living there didn't speak of in public. Too many people disbelieved during that era, fearing that they would be thought strange. This home was a favorite place for hauntings and activities involving mischievous ghosts. I was told that, oftentimes, curtains would open and close without human assistance, strange smells would permeate the halls, babies would laugh at imaginary guests, and sounds of footsteps and chains would awaken the family from a dead sleep at night. It was probably a good thing that I didn't know of such things that first contact night.

Guardian Angels

Years passed, and though I had a healthy interest in ghosts, goblins, and anything strange, there were no physical manifestations to elicit the gooseflesh of days gone by. Intuitive by nature, there were, however, instances of psychic phenomena of a mild nature in my life. But even so, I've never once seen a ghost. That's not to say, however, that they've not been around me … or that I won't see one in the future.

Other people see and hear them around me from time to time. A co-worker from my past advised me once that he saw an "angel" standing over me as I typed at my computer on a deadline-oriented project that was crucial to the well being of many people. When he came closer, the entity disappeared. (This might explain the strange feeling of being watched when no one is there to watch me—particularly when I'm working at the computer on a manuscript. It's as though someone is reading over my shoulder—but there is never anyone there when I turn to look.)

At other negative time periods I've been through, it has seemed as though this angel, or ghost, or guardian—whatever one chooses to call such a being—has shown a protective nature. It locked my unlocked door to an interested suitor one cold snowy evening. This person came to call on me and "my ghost" would not allow entrance. The lock on the door was in the unlocked position but the door would not open. I struggled to open it. My intended suitor also attempted to open it from the other side—to no avail. The door would not budge. It finally did open as I chose not to give up trying until I was successful. I went with this person out into the snowy night, not heeding the now obvious warning—but thinking about it. Suffice it to say that I should have listened to the message. The relationship was not a good one. It turned out that this person was not to be trusted. My ghost did not like this deception and would not let deceit pass without a fight.

My daughter, who is more intuitive than I in many ways, can actually hear ghosts. It was a surprise to me, one evening, to learn this about her after I'd been involved in a minor fender-bender on slippery railroad tracks in Timonium, Maryland. Traffic was heavy, rain was drizzling, and a lady could not stop her car as she rolled over the metal tracks. She hit me from the rear. Nothing significant. No damage. No injury. The incident upset her more than me. When I returned home and entered the house, the first thing my daughter asked was, "What's this about railroad tracks? What happened?" It seemed that she'd heard the ghost whisper of railroad tracks. She couldn't get the whole story, just the words: railroad tracks. This was my first indication that my daughter was cognizant of the protecting entity living with us in a way that affected her personally.

Some years later she told me that the ghost had protected her as well when a boyfriend had been alone in our home with her. Though she would not tell what transpired, the incident was one that required outside intervention to maintain her safety. All she would tell me was, "The ghost made himself known, Mom. That's all you need to know." (Though I was cringing inside about what incident could make the ghost manifest, this was, indeed, something I didn't want to know.)

Still another protective period came when negative marital episodes became prevalent in our household. My spouse (at that time) would turn on all the lights in the home out of fear of the strange happenings that seemed to occur only when he was alone in the house. My other half would see a person sitting at my computer (who looked like me, he'd rant) when I was not home. The television would switch to a particular channel of white, noisy buzz every time it was turned on when my daughter and I were not home. Any attempt on his part to change the channel would bring it right back to the buzzing one after he'd returned to a comfortable chair. Varied things, done to annoy, would be commonplace.

Unhappy in that marriage, my daughter and I used to have quite a giggle over it. These things were never done to us—only to the person whom the ghost felt malice toward. Eventually this spouse left our lives and things returned to normal. No ghost for many years.

Time passed, and later, I was warned not to enter into a particular real estate arrangement by bursting light bulbs. This happened as I wrote out the first check and a second time, the day we moved in. I disregarded the warning and negative issues plagued us the entire time we lived there. Not ghostly issues, but daily living issues. I've since decided that I need to clearly listen to these warnings. Someone out there is watching over me and knows better than I do what the best course of action is! Ghostly interventions can be very good things in many cases.

So you see, I haven't seen orbs in my photos, filmy figures on the stairs, flying dishes, nor have I been witness to any significant haunting. But I have some experience. Some. And I have a feeling that as I write this book, I will gain much more.

I hope you enjoy the following stories!

—D. P. Roseberry
www.roseberrybooks.com

Special Author Note: *Just a little warning before we continue. Many consider cemeteries holy places. When visiting any cemetery, please be respectful, for the sake of the living and in respect for the dead. Whether active cemeteries are public or private, most have posted visiting hours. To keep yourself on the right side of the law, this author recommends visiting only during the hours when a cemetery is posted as open to the public, unless you obtain explicit permission to do otherwise.*

Respect is, of course, also important when discussing, visiting, investigating, etc. all of the locations listed within this book. Please take all legal precautions and maintain courtesy to those you come in contact with.

Introduction

A Brief Historical Overview of Phoenixville and Valley Forge, Pennsylvania

There are reasons that ghosts reside in Phoenixville and Valley Forge.

Photo. Only. Copyright 1905 by the Rotograph Co.
Entrance to Reeves Park, Phoenixville, Pa

A historical postcard view of Reeves Park in Phoenixville, circa 1910. The park is a central meeting area for current events and community activities. It is located adjacent to the very haunted Phoenixville Public Library.

Phoenixville

Phoenixville, located within an easy commute of the thriving Philadelphia, this integral Chester County town on the west banks of the Schuylkill River has been collecting ghosts since the

1730s. Around that time, the Lenni-Lenape people living in the area were affiliated with the Iroquois Confederation and were typically hunters, gatherers, and farmers. European explorers found these (mostly) peaceful people by the waterway and began their quest to settle among them, many being religious refugees from across the ocean.

Moses Coates, an explorer of the area, persuaded a miller named James Starr, in 1731, to buy land on the south side of French Creek. He did buy the land and built the first gristmill, allowing farmers the ability to use a local mill rather than transporting crops down river to Plymouth. Starr built his own house on what is now called Main Street, just north of Bridge Street, in 1732. As business grew for the mill area, a settlement also grew.

As a sidenote, gristmills, while useful, oftentimes made the locals in the towns where they were built very nervous. Some believed that gristmill owners were in league with the Devil. This belief arose from the fact that, from time to time, gristmills were known to mysteriously explode in all-consuming infernos. People didn't linger long around them!

There were still Indian issues to make life dangerous during Phoenixville's early history. In 1755, the French and Indian Wars provided settlers with disquieting Indian attacks, even though fifteen volunteers fought under General Braddock in attempts to halt the aggression.

There were approximately 450 people living in Phoenixville at the time the American Revolution began, including Mennonites, Quakers, and even a few slaves. Wagons brought American soldiers to the churches, meetinghouses, and taverns of the area.

Burial grounds housing the Revolution's dead can be found throughout the townships.

Unfortunately for the area, the American forces were defeated at the Revolutionary Brandywine battle. Following that defeat, Washington crossed his troops to the east bank of the Schuylkill, and the British under General Howe marched through Chester County in pursuit. Arriving with 14,000 troops and camping along Nutt Road between the Bull Tavern (now LaTaverna) and Bridge Street, they were aggressive and warlike, vandalizing every house and business in the area.

History of the Fountain Inn—the farthest point that the British reached during the Revolutionary War—tells us that the town, at that time, was called Gordonsford, named after a squatter named Gordon (a most unpleasant fellow, according to some, living in a cave with a harem of women). Benjamin Longstretch and Louis Wernwag, the manufacturers of iron at the French Creek Works, decided to rename the town one evening upon seeing the hot iron furnace light up the sky with blazing magnificence. The great Egyptian mythology bird, the Phoenix, came to mind as this was a bird that regained new strength out of its own ashes. The Borough of Phoenixville was incorporated in 1849.

Phoenixville today has a population of about 16,000 people—and an unknown population of ghostly residents.

Valley Forge

Valley Forge's most memorable time was during the Revolutionary War in 1777-1778—though the associated memories are filled with hardship, suffering, and death. Oddly enough, not military acts of war, but disease claimed nearly one in ten soldiers during cold snowy winters. Dysentery and typhus overwhelmed the masses.

Because Valley Forge, named after a small village sitting where the Valley Creek moved into the Schuylkill River, was at a high elevation with water barriers for protection, it was perceived to be an area with military advantage—attacking soldiers would have to assault up hill. The area was stocked heavily with supplies for soldiers.

CONTINENTAL ARMY HUT, Valley Forge, Pa.

A historical postcard view of a typical Continental Army Hut in Valley Forge. These huts can be seen throughout the park and were the only protection soldiers had from the weather during the wartime encampment.

Huts were built to the specifications of General Washington, providing not only shelter, but a stone fireplace for warmth and cooking. However, the huts proved unhealthy structures—cold and wet—not at all conducive to maintaining a strong and healthy army. This was especially the case since, once the British learned about the cache of goods at Valley Forge (after the Battle of Brandywine), the stocks were taken and the area burned. Clothing and feeding the tired and sick soldiers was the downfall of the army.

Typical weather plagued the troops as they struggled to stay alive that winter, with temperatures dipping into the twenties, and rain and snow hammering their spirits. Though makeshift hospitals were set up in area structures, there was a lack of personnel to staff them, few medical supplies to assist recoveries, and this quickly became an unfavorable place that managed to spread even more disease.

The first hospital to be built for the Valley Forge soldiers was at historic Yellow Springs (about ten miles west of Valley Forge on the far side of Phoenixville). Three hundred men were treated there.

Sanitation issues brought much death to Valley Forge soldiers and their valued livestock. Further, rotting horse flesh contributed to the already horrendous health hazards nearly as much as the scarcity of supplies. Water was polluted by human waste and neglected huts housed un-circulated air carrying germs and sickness. Illness and death were evident everywhere. A miasma of illnesses and the specter of slow, lingering death crept among the suffering soldiers during the short, bone-chilling winter days, and long, bleak nights at Valley Forge. Even as the winter turned to spring, Washington was informed by the medical professionals that 1,000 men were too sick to fight.

It is unknown how many succumbed to the serious ills plaguing the forces at Valley Forge. Most died in nearby impromptu hospitals. Therefore, actual gravesites are few (if any) across the fields of war. But there are 3,000 estimated dead—enough warrant the ghosts that walk the countryside.

The Ghosts of Phoenixville and Valley Forge

Ghosts reside within these tales; and beyond through steel and war.

Be still, and hear the quiet sounds—whispers soft and sure.

See roses spin, hear counters tic, as nights grow dark and old.

See soldiers run across the fields, their stories far from told.

Know buzzing bees and door bell chimes; see movie terrors, too.

Hear children laugh in stairwells dark, and clocks with lights bright blue.

Of course, see shadows, dark and fierce, that walk among the dead.

Their footsteps heard both high and low, bring living people dread.

A book will fly right off the shelf, a horse's hooves will sound.

The miners digging tunnels deep will surely come around.

For all are here in Phoenixville and Valley Forge to see.

The ghosts and haunts of days gone by, have yarns for you to read.

Please join me now and read these tales of haunts (both day and night).

For spirits of these towns prevail, their stories may delight.

—D. P. Roseberry

And So
the Hauntings Begin...
Phoenixville

The Phoenixville Area
Chamber of Commerce

171 East Bridge Street
Phoenixville, PA 19460
610-933-3070

What better place to start than in the heart of the business
and commerce sections for the historic community of Phoenixville,
Pennsylvania. The Phoenixville Area Chamber of Commerce has
been at its current location at 171 East Bridge Street since the
1950s. Kim Cooley, the President of the Chamber, advises that

the organization has been working as business advocate for local organizations for about eighty years. She was an integral part of the plan to get the current Chamber office up and running. Representing business interests of northeastern Chester County and western Montgomery County, the Chamber is an organization that works for the overall benefit of the business community.

Oh, and did I forget to mention that the Chamber is haunted? I assured Kim—and she agreed—that ghosts are good for business. I'd visited the Chamber hoping to hear gossip about ghosts in other historic buildings in the area, but hadn't expected to find one so quickly in this first location.

Footsteps to Work By

"I talk to 'em," says busy Kim Cooley as she talks to me and conducts Chamber business at the same time. "When I'm alone, that's who I'm talkin' to."

It seems that a ghost paces the upstairs rooms as Kim and her assistant conduct their daily business downstairs. She advised that since she's been there (about a year at the time of this interview), she'd been hearing the footsteps pace back and forth above them. "Whoever's here knows more than anyone else knows about me!" she continued with a light-hearted laugh—a joking giggle that made me smile. "We just kinda have fun with it," she said.

Looking around the building, I saw nothing that seemed especially haunting or out of the ordinary. It was a normal office with normal office paraphernalia situated about. I continued to watch Kim work—now taking photos of a small dog for a fundraiser she'd planned. People came and went as we talked but I wasn't hearing the ghost in question on her upper floor.

"Are the footsteps you hear heavy footsteps?" I asked.

"It's a man. It's definitely a man—not even a heavy woman. You can tell by the way he walks. It's the heel hitting the floor. Women don't walk like that. Its more like a...a man!" she said with a laugh. She was confident and matter-of-fact. There was no doubt. There was no questioning the phenomena. There was a male ghost pacing the upstairs floors of the Chamber of Commerce.

Kim isn't alone listening to the ghostly footsteps. Her assistant, Trish, has heard them as well. She was not particularly excited about the phenomena. "I've been here about seven years, and it's been more recent that we've heard the steps. Since Kim came."

"It's me!" added Kim. "I bring them out. I'm serious! It makes perfect sense because of the way I talk out loud when no one is here. I'm talking constantly."

Trish is nodding now. "Yes, I know. I talk like that, too, when nobody's here."

Both Kim and Trish have had other paranormal experiences outside the Chamber office, as well. A ghost of a family cat stays near to Trish, though she was hesitant to tell me about it. "One night, I was in bed and I woke up, not being able to move my feet. I had two cats—one lays at my head, one lays on her little pillow in between my husband and I. But I couldn't move my feet. Something was lying on my feet! I truly think it was my deceased cat."

"But back to the footsteps," said Trish. "I've heard them up-stairs and every once in a while, I think they are in the closet—because things fall sometime when there's no reason for them to be falling." She opened the closet for me to peer into. It was well organized and I clearly saw that for an object to fall, there had to be someone—or something—pushing it.

Both Kim and Trish have heard the footsteps at the same time, giving further credence to the ghostly inhabitant. But neither has heard them while actually upstairs themselves—only from the downstairs office with the steps sounding over their heads.

Kim advised me, "Wouldn't surprise me if I brought them with me."

"Why?" I asked. "Do you feel them anywhere else?"

Both women were nodding about this.

Ladies of the Chamber and Their Other Haunts!

"Oh yeah. She's nodding about shadows of animals," Kim said, motioning towards Trish. "I literally see silhouettes. Around me. I could be anywhere. Out of the corner of my eye I'll see a shadow, and there's nothing there when I look. But it's there. Something's following me." She paused. "The shadows don't bother me. I guess I've been dealing with them so long, they just don't …"

Taking me down into the recesses of the Chamber's creepy basement, we all felt a strange sensation, yet no specific manifestation erupted for us to see—nor has anything ever been witnessed from this part of the building. Just a tingly feeling whenever going down the stairs. Both Kim and Trish get the creeps in the cramped and dimly lit basement—and I can understand that. With its rock walls showing the dark shadows cast by my flashlight and cracked cement floor making our movements uneven, this basement was truly a creepy place.

The ladies were animated now because both felt manifestations quite regularly.

Kim chimed in (upstairs and away from the creepy basement), "When I was a kid, there was a woman who would stand over my bed all the time. She was dressed in old clothing and held a tray. I can remember being a little kid and saying, 'She's here again, Mom.' She had her hair tied back in a bun, dark clothing, a tray, and ruffles at her wrists. I didn't get the servant feeling, I got more the caretaker feeling. I can remember vividly opening my eyes to see her, and I can still see her today, standing by my bed from time to time."

It seems that people who are open to psychic phenomena tend to have it in varied parts of their lives.

But What About Right Now?

Oddly enough, activity has stirred even more at the Chamber since my initial interviews. Speaking to Kim, she says, "Oh, you haven't heard the latest! It's really creepy, but I have no proof!" It seems that she's been getting telephone messages from beyond—or at least from some unidentifiable place. When she plays back the recorder, she hears frantic whispering but cannot make out the words. Later, when she tried to play the message for someone else to hear, the message had disappeared from the machine. This happened twice in the prior days.

So a special investigation was scheduled to be conducted by the Chester County Paranormal Research Society that would delve into these strange events at the Chamber—and I was going to be part of it.

The Investigation

I'd like to say that the whole investigation of the Chamber of Commerce began as a dark and stormy Friday night, but this was not the case. In fact, it was so hot and humid that perspiration was a constant companion as the group entered into the Chamber at roughly five p.m. carrying equipment of all shapes and sizes. This, being my first investigation, was a marvel to me. I'd certainly seen the television programs showing how these examinations of the paranormal took place, but I was not prepared for the significant scientific protocol that would be imperative for a true and realistic research study.

As equipment was being set up (cameras, video recorders, etc.), I was assigned to the upstairs graphing team. It was our job to map out the Chamber in a floor plan that would display all electrical items—light switches, power plates, lights, appliances (i.e. air conditioners), or any other thing that might affect an investigation. Once the graph was finished, we set about using EMF meters (see glossary for explanation) to take base readings. These readings were then written on the graph. A base EMF reading taken throughout the rooms involved would give us a comparison to later readings that we would be taking during our investigation.

Researching graph statistical data was not a particular eye-opener, but I could tell that it would be valuable—just how valuable, I was only beginning to understand. After the graphing, I spent the rest of my evening of research with my mouth open in

I-can't-believe-I'm-seeing-this awe. Even securing base readings was interesting. It was also our job to debunk as we went along, so readings that showed high numbers around any area where electrical current was present for the right reasons (i.e. outlets, etc.) were closely monitored whenever our meters began to beep. The interesting part, to me, was how the energy seemed to follow us through the process. So many areas, where there was no rational/scientific cause for electrical current to be, showed energy readings. It was as though whatever was there from the other world was very curious about what we were doing. At one time, the meter would be flashing an indication of energy presence, and in the very next minute, at the same place and under the same conditions, there was nothing showing. It was definitely the kind of thing that could make the hair stand up on end.

Once the preliminaries of the investigation were completed, the actual investigation began. This was where time had to be put in. One of the research phases is called (for our group) the vigil. Sitting in the midst of the camera equipment, wandering around with the EMF meters to take readings, and noting changes—which were too numerous to mention—are all quiet, time-consuming tasks. Much of what happens seems to be invisible to most of us.

At one point, however, another investigator came up the stairs to tell us that the orb activity was quite elaborate—displayed on the downstairs monitor from the upstairs cameras.

I'd not seen an orb before, though I'd looked hard for one. So I decided that I would go back downstairs to see what the monitors were showing. I was flabbergasted. And I could not stop saying, "Oh my *God!*"

The television monitor in front of me, which was wired to the camera equipment on the second level of the Chamber, was alive with orb activity. All sizes were whooshing through the room—some twinkling like starlight, some bright, some soft in glow. All were traveling so that a tail of energy spun out behind them as they disappeared from the camera's lens to parts unknown. It looked like a major traffic hub of paranormal activity! I was so excited I could barely contain myself. There, in front of my eyes, were orbs—scientific proof (to me...) that something was out there beyond our ability to see.

But what is an orb? This question has been asked of me several times during my story collection. According to the Co-founder, Mark Sarro, of the Chester County Paranormal Research Society:

> Orbs in the simplest explanation are spherical shaped anomalies that can be caused by various reasons. An orb usually appears in a photograph and/or in video. They can be dust particles that refract light back to the camera and illuminate the particles, making them appear luminescent. These orbs are usually perfectly round and transparent (when captured in a still photograph). The kind of camera and distance of the lens from the flash can greatly affect the possibility as to whether or not the camera will capture a "dust orb." Digital cameras especially can produce these effects as well as another type of orb, which is the result of "pixel dropout." This is a result of the camera not being able to process the image fully, and literally, a single pixel may drop out of the image. These orbs will appear solid and white, and almost like a pinhole has been placed in the picture. When you

look closer at the image (with the help of computer-based software) the "orb" will be square. This type of orb is common with older digital cameras and those at a lower mega-pixelation. Other types of naturally recurring orbs are a result of refracted light from a drop of water (rain, snow etc).

After you have ruled out these natural types of orbs, what remains may very well be paranormal. There are many theories as to what paranormal orbs may be. Some believe that they are ghosts or spirits, and others have gone so far as to say that they are angels. Still others believe that they are anomalous energy and nothing more then that. Energy, in it's rawest form, is spherical and usually emits it's own light source. In still photographs, orbs may have a trail or be blurrier in the image, and in video, they will have an erratic pattern and usually defy gravity, making it known that you are not looking at a dust particle.

The size of these orbs may vary, but most common are the ones that are smaller in size and usually only seen when revealed in a photograph or video. Chester County Paranormal Research Society gravitates towards the theory that orbs are anomalous paranormal energy and not "ghosts or spirits" caught on film or in a picture. My own personal theory regarding these phenomena is that if paranormal orbs are present, then it may be a sign that other paranormal activity may be present—i.e., ghosts, spirits, or other activity.

Dave Juliano of South Jersey Ghost Research reports that:

One of the leading theories concerning what orbs are and the one that I lean towards the most is that they are not the spirit at all. The orb is the energy being transferred from a source (i.e. power lines, heat energy, batteries, people, etc.) to the spirit so they can manifest. This may not even be a conscious thing the spirit is doing, just a natural way they get their energy. This would explain why the orbs are round balls. According to the laws of Physics, energy being transferring like that would assume the natural shape of a sphere. This theory can also be tied into the EMF readings we get during spirit activity.

I've heard it said that famous psychic Sylvia Browne believes that orbs are angels, and that the circular objects picked up by our high-tech camera equipment represent the energy of these entities. It seems pretty conclusive that orbs are energy, but not so clear as to what the energy is. Is it propelling a being? Is it an angel? I just know that after seeing it for myself, I'm quite sure that it is paranormal.

Later in the evening, a vigil of the upstairs haunted room continued. Our group, made up of varied individuals who have varied sensitivities to the paranormal, were situated around a large table in the middle of the room. The camera was running. An EMF meter sat on the table, turned on and flashing red to indicate a constant high range of energy in the room with us. We remained quiet and in waiting mode. I watched everyone closely. This was interesting.

It wasn't long before two members of the group felt feather-light touches on their arms, like a small breeze ruffling the hairs on the forearm. There was no moving air source in the room—and the temperature (taken continually by a thermometer on the table) was approximately eighty-two degrees. (A window air conditioner in the adjoining room was the method of cooling for the upstairs and was not at high level.) Another member felt someone touch the cross tattoo on her arm, as if investigating it.

It appeared that all the physical activity was taking place on one side of the room. At an appropriate interval, the group sitting on the active side of the room switched places with those on the inactive side of the room.

I was now in the middle of the active area. All was still ... but not for long.

Wearing open-toed sandals, jeans, and a t-shirt, the only skin exposed to the air were my toes and my forearms. I could feel (though thinking back now, I'm not sure anymore) a movement of air across my arms as they rested on the chair arms. Looking around, I tried to note whether anyone was moving. I looked through the doorway out into the adjoining room and thought about the air conditioner out there. I wasn't sure if there was air movement or not, but it felt like there was indeed a coolness to the air around my right arm—not a dramatic cool, just a bit cooler than the warm air in the room. I pulled my attention from the air and tried to relax.

It was then that I felt the cool air at my feet, on my bare toes. I was sure of the air this time. And then, as though a piece of human hair was being dragged across my skin, I felt a tickling sensation across my toes. I looked down but nothing was there. Yet I knew that I'd felt something. Gooseflesh came up on my arms.

My mind reeled with thoughts of this research: if one considers that footsteps are being heard when no one is there, orbs are highly abundant on video camera, EMF readings are active, and physical manifestations are apparent, I'd say there's a being of some sort at the Chamber of Commerce. Ghost? Spirit? Angel? Energy? I'm not sure what's there. And those at the Chamber have no idea who could possibly be haunting their premises. But somebody or something is there as far as I'm concerned.

Serenitea

10 South Main Street
Phoenixville, PA 19460

Sheila Cain-Coghill, owner of the former Serenitea—a lovely tea shop that, until June of 2006, was located at 10 South Main Street, has had a haunting or two in her shop.

The clock radio has a blue light that the Serenitea ghost seemed to like.

Of course, I might have suspected that she knew of hauntings. Sheila's shop was filled with quiet character and mystery. The shop's inviting front room held a wall of teas and a display case of tarot cards and varied mystical items—things that make you wide-eyed with wonder, and thirsty for really good tea. Between the front room and the back room was a doorway of beads—more mystery. Through the curtain of beads, one steps into a cozy tearoom that is both welcoming and charming. Under the right circumstances, this would be the perfect place for a ghost to lounge. Sheila had tea waiting for me.

Bells and Radios

It was here, over steaming rose tea, that I learned of the Serenitea haunted clock-radio.

But to begin with, Sheila talked of the entrance bells to the shop. They rang when no one was there or entering the shop. She'd be in the back of the shop brewing tea or taking a call when the front door chiming bells would ring as though a customer or visitor had dropped in for a spot of afternoon tea. Quickly, Sheila would move through the beaded curtain to the front of the shop, only to find the shop deserted and the door secure and shut. Sometimes, there would be a slight movement that she would catch from the corner of her eye—but nothing or no one would be in the room.

"See the pyramid-shaped stereo?" she questioned me. I did. It was a modern design stereo, shaped like a pyramid, lit with an alluring blue light at the top, and had a clock inset. "The ghost really likes the blue light. If I turn that off at night when I leave, it doesn't like it."

I frowned. Did ghosts listen to music or tell time? I shrugged, "What...does the ghost turn it back on?"

"Oh yes," advised Sheila. "It'll turn it back on. I went out to run an errand once and turned off the radio. I ran into some friends, chit chatted; came back and the radio was playing." She stopped and looked directly into my eyes. "It works on remote, you know. Only by remote. And it was on."

I merely nodded, pulling my eyes from hers to look at the blue-lit clock on the stereo.

"So," said Sheila, "I just thought I'd leave it on all the time."

She doesn't know who the ghost is and hasn't been able find out at this point. The building, being various things to various people over time, could have picked up a ghost anywhere along its historic line, she thought. She's looking into it as she researches some of the other town haunts.

The Black Rock Tunnel

(Part of the Phoenixville Railroad Station)

Sheila Cain-Coghill told me about a big hill here that was cut through by a railway, creating the Black Rock Tunnel. Built in 1837, the 1,932 foot long tunnel was the longest tunnel in the United States at that time, and the third of its kind to be constructed.

Sheila said, "We bought our house up on Tunnel Hill and I

was describing it to my mother—where it was. And she said 'Oh, you're living on Tunnel Hill'. I'd been puzzled and replied, 'how do you know that?' Well, it seems that my mother and sisters used to come down from Reading on the train. They would get off where there used to be a station—over by where the Gay Street Bridge is now. And the tunnel was a huge deal because they could have train service available—only the trains couldn't climb the hill. They needed to have a tunnel. But, they couldn't seem to dig one. No matter what they did, they couldn't get it done. This is how Irish ended up in Phoenixville. They brought the Irish over to dig the tunnel."

"It's some kind of peculiar rock—which is why it's called the Black Rock Tunnel. They imported Irish miners, and they were able to do the job. In the course of the task, however, there was a cave in and an explosion—not unusual in mining situations, because digging a tunnel was like digging a mine. The whole crew was killed."

Sheila stopped to continue sipping her tea and then looked up at me. "They're still there in the tunnel. Apparently, they just show up from time to time."

It doesn't surprise me, upon further research, that these miners are showing up at the tunnel. A study listed by the American Museum of Natural History shows that teeth and bone fragments have been found in the rock at Black Rock Tunnel, as well as skull, dorso lumbar, femur, and pelvis fibula and fragments. Creepy, yes?

But the tales do not end here. Still another story—or lack of story—comes to light around this eeire tunnel. Andrea Martinishn of the Ghost Tours of Phoenixville advises that, after talking with the Phoenixville Historical Society, the lines of truth and urban legend blur even further. The Society says that this incident never happened! There was no collapse and no dead miners. So if this ghostly incident never took place, who—or what—is responsible for the strange stories and happenings affiliated with the Black Rock Tunnel?

Well, maybe things are not as creepy as it seems according to author, researcher, and editor Jeff Snyder. He wondered: Who left the bones behind? Did the American Museum of Natural History actually make that study? And if they did conduct the research, what rocks would they have been studying? Debris removed from the collapse?

After a bit of "digging" on his own, he uncovered another story. "The American Museum of Natural History did find the bones during an 1866 survey conducted at the tunnel," he advised. "However, they were fossil bones belonging to a crocodile-like creature, a phytosaur named Rutiodon carolinensis living way back in the Late Triassic period, roughly 200 million years ago."

So who or what haunts the Black Rock Tunnel? Jeff's suggestion? "If you run across any spectres with large, toothy grins at the Black Rock Tunnel ...don't smile back!" I'm thinking it may be a good idea to run!

The Phoenixville Mansion House

37 East Bridge Street
Phoenixville, PA 19460
telephone: 610-933-9962
Free tarot card readings from 6-9:30 Third Wednesday of every month by appt. only. (A ghostly restaurant with tarot card readings must be a real treat!)

One place I've enjoyed visiting (many times) because of the friendly staff and good food has been the Phoenixville Mansion House. It has a charm that feels quaint and yet modern—this, despite the fact that the Mansion was first licensed to serve as an inn and to furnish food, drink, and lodging for travelers back in 1850. I always smile at the sign on the side of the building (by the parking lot) that welcomes autos, horses, and carriages. A stable was attached to the building so that overnight travelers had a place to tend their horses—you can still see the O hooks that the townspeople used for securing their four-legged rides.

Of course, anyone who frequents the Mansion House has heard of the ghosts there. In fact, the stories are so interesting, that the owners tell about their invisible friends right on their menu. My visit this night, then, was to be a quick appetizer meal, some chat with the staff, and a copy of the history shown on their menu. I never expected what happened to happen. I was a collector of stories—not a participant in hauntings!

I started with a general fact-finding interview to discover exactly what happened historically with this fine restaurant/inn. According to the owners (JoVin Enterprises—Jodie, Vinny, and Lil):

The first original bar room and dining room was located in the basement, in the rear portion of the building. The original dining room sign still remains on the lower level door. On May 18, 1887, the bar room, by order of the law, was moved to its present area, located on the first floor street level (Bridge Street). The wooden table, that was used to prepare dinners, is now used to separate the two dining rooms. You can see the original cut marks in the wood.

In 1910, the Mansion House was lighted with electricity and is still heated with steam today. On July 3, 1998, the Mansion House was purchased by JoVin Enterprises. We invested every dollar made right back into the business. During the first four years of hard work, we made many improvements while preserving its historical charm. Once the inside was renovated, we painted the outside, restoring the old time signs to the exact measurements, colors, and sayings. Our business had developed by serving dinners, holding banquets, and hosting historic bus tours. We were very proud of our accomplishments. Our staff and our customers became our dear friends.

On August 4, 2002, the Mansion House had a devastating fire, with the smoke and soot totally engulfing the entire first floor of the restaurant. Homes were lost; jobs were lost. Thank God, no lives were lost! We're not used to defeat. So, we began again and it took us two long years. Some things have changed, out of necessity, but our charm, hospitality, kindness, and sincerity remains the same.

Of course, among the things that remained the same were the ghosts. And many of the staff—and now me—have seen the proof of that! Their menu continues:

The "Sundance Kid," (his real name was Harry Longabaugh) was born in 1867 and lived with his family in Port Providence. He moved, along with his family to Phoenixville in 1880. The "Kid's" family home was located at 354 Church Street, Phoenixville.

At thirteen years of age, he worked with horses on the E. Vincent Farm off Route 113 and 401. At the age of fifteen, the "Kid" settled in Colorado, Montana, and Sundance, Wyoming, which was where he got into trouble. He stole a horse, a gun, and a saddle. After being apprehended, he spent eighteen months in jail and was dubbed "The Sundance Kid."

After a history of lawlessness, he moved to Argentina and started a new life. In 1901, Sundance and his wife, Ethel Place, returned to Phoenixville to visit family and stayed here at the Mansion House.

This very story was told to the Historical Society by Donna Ernst. The "Sundance Kid" was her husband's great uncle. Donna Ernst has written a book on the subject, "Sundance, My Uncle."

Presently, while working the restaurant, since 1998, we have heard someone opening the door with footsteps across the floor, only to look and see nothing. Psychics have felt the presence of other guests, back from the Civil War, still roaming the kitchen, dining room, and hallways.

During restoration, after the fire, several workers felt someone lightly brushing their hair back; doors continually closed or opened with no one there, and the strong scent of cinnamon was present in certain areas, even after being cleaned with pine cleaner. Even though the sounds, scents, and touches have been non-threatening, some of the workers refused to return to work.

A Rose By Any Other Name May Not Turn As Sweetly

This was all very interesting. Ghost stories always are. But when you mixed in the current and daily occurrences of the people standing in front of you, stories become realities; and the gooseflesh creeps.

It was that way, for me, with the rose.

I'd, again, like to say that it started on dark and stormy night (as I'd hoped with the Chamber investigation), but that wasn't the case. It was bright, sunny, and hot as I strolled into the Phoenixville Mansion House with my tape recorder and camera in

This shot was taken while the rose was in motion, turning in a complete circle in its vase.

hand. The flow of cool air hit me quickly, a relief from the stale humid air just outside the door. The bar room was welcoming with laughing customers around the bar and busy employees tending to customer needs throughout the establishment. Tony, the Bar Manager, was on duty this night. With the Mansion House for over fifteen years, he was a cool pro—delivering drinks and food with ease and seeming to know what a customer wanted before being asked. Zackery was on deck as well, young and sharp—and willing to talk about ghosts from the first moment I asked. I started with Zack.

Zack was the person who first mentioned Table Two and the rose. It was actually a surprise; I hadn't expected to actually see a manifestation of the paranormal. I'd planned to hear about hauntings. Zack told me that a single rose in a bud vase turned nearly every evening. But on this day, the rose had been turning off and on all day long. I didn't really understand exactly what he meant, and was trying to digest the turning of a rose in some fashion when another employee called out, "It's doing it right now, if you wanna see it!" By then, several employees were about and beckoning me into the dining room—to Table Two.

The rose was beckoning me, too. Moving off the bar stool, just barely aware that my photographer husband was right behind me, I followed Andee, one of the boisterous waitresses, to the quaint but elegant dining room. Somehow, in those few seconds, my mind had wisped away the sounds of the bar, replacing the welcome noise with a silence inside me that thumped like a heartbeat. I'd heard stories. I'd played with Ouija Boards. I'd felt the presence of the otherworld. But I'd never actually seen a manifestation like this. I was about to. Just steps away.

My heartbeat sped with each pace.

In the dining room, I noted that every table had a small green glass bud vase containing one artificial red rose placed with stately grace in the middle of the table. I moved to the table they were ushering me to with wide eyes. Standing there looking at the rose, I could feel the struggle within me. The little voice that so often haunts us was haunting me right now. It was saying: *Can't be. Must be a reason. Not real.*

But that kind of thinking would not bode well here—not here where the natural was unnatural, where the living were not the only ones enjoying the company of others. Here, there were...ghosts.

"That is so cool," I stammered. And it was. There, in the center of the table, sat the tall, skinny vase with the red rose turning inside—the flower moving in full circles. It's red petals faced me, looking real and lovely, and then turned away so that only the smooth side of green leaves with a soft flush of red could be seen. It turned and turned with the same speed and consistency of a motorized machine.

My first instinct was to look about for ceiling fans and floor vents. Andee, Jason, and Katie, three of the employees standing with me, knew what I was looking for, and nodded knowingly to each other. I was not the first to question the air about the phenomena. But there were no ceiling fans, and though there was an air conditioning vent nearby, there was no flow of air currently coming from it. I moved cautiously forward, my eyes glued to the rose as it slowly continued its journey around and around. Reaching to wrap my arms around the area to see if I could feel an outside air source strong enough to move the flower, I struggled for understanding. No air. And if there were, I'd have been blocking the source.

Yet, there was a cold spot at one side of the flower. I shivered. This was like the stories I'd watched on television and in the movies. The cold spot that indicated that one was not alone, that there were invisible beings standing near—breathing and projecting a chill that touched the back of the neck and brought gooseflesh to the arms. The employees had not felt the cold spot before and clamored to experience it. It was agreed that, indeed, one area by the flower was colder than the room air and that the coolness came from no visible source.

We experimented with moving the flower from one table to another and one vase to another, but the flower would not turn in any other location. The flower and vase needed to be on Table Two—together. Andee said, "The consistent thing we can count on is that flower turning. Even if there's no heat, no air, no nothing, that flower turns." Then she added, "I don't think you should mess with him."

A Breezy Evening With Jeremy

After a time, I managed to pull myself away from the rose, so that I could talk a bit more with Tony about some of the other things that were happening at The Mansion House. The rose was just one item on a list of many odd occurrences to consider.

Tony advised me that it all began for him back when he first began working at the Mansion House (in approximately 1992). Downstairs one evening, at the close of business and as he was bringing beer up to stock the bar, a strange cool breeze came up behind him. It lifted the back of his hair from his neck. He turned on the stairwell to see what could have caused such a wind in a closed area. Nothing. He saw nothing. But he felt something. "I was new here at the time and all by myself. I just locked up and ran home!" He added that when one was alone at night in the Mansion House, the creaks and noises make things very creepy. The next day following the breezy first floor incident, Tony contacted the owner to talk of the uncomfortable feelings and things that he'd felt. He was told, "Oh, that's just Jeremy—he's not going to hurt you!"

My eyes widened. Aha! A name. A person. A story. I was about to find out who was haunting the inn. Apparently, through the ghost grapevine, other folks in earlier years had felt presences, too, and other employees had felt the cold and breezy downstairs. They'd also seen the rose (which still intrigued me). But I was curious, now, about Jeremy.

Andee came forth to tell me the story. It began some years ago when a blind woman came with her husband to enjoy the food provided by the House. And where were they seated? Table Two, of course! The woman said to the server, "Do you know that you have ghosts here?" The server (and everyone else on staff) did, indeed, know of the ghosts even then, and told the woman about the ghost of Table Two. But the woman frowned up at the server with blind eyes. "No," she said pointing to a serving station at a nearby area by the kitchen. "He is over there by the side station." It was wondered by staff then—and staff now—how a blind woman even knew that there was what they called a "side station" where she'd pointed. The woman's husband took her by the arm and led her to the station, where she had about a twenty-minute conversation with the ghost.

One of the Mansion House ghosts was identified. The ghost, Jeremy, told the blind woman that he was a Civil War soldier who had been killed at the age of twenty-one. He described himself as six-foot-two with blond hair and blue eyes. (Andee felt—and I do believe she may be right—that he sounded quite appealing. It is comical how light and airy the staff makes their ghosts sound. These are friendly and welcome ghosts!) Now, in this time, the ghost in the dining room turning the rose is called by name—Jeremy.

Food at the Mansion House is Worth Ordering—
Even if You're A Ghost!

But the hauntings do not stop with sweet Jeremy and his romantic turning rose. Another ghost at the Mansion House has had a pretty good hankering for a roast beef hoagie—dry, on a long roll—at least seven or eight times each year. And to make it more interesting, this ghost has mastered the computer ordering system. I'm sure that most of you understand the usage of computers in restaurants and bars today. The server uses the computer to order the food by touching the screen; the data is transferred to a computer station in the kitchen where the kitchen staff prepares the food for the customer.

At the Mansion House, the kitchen staff is very careful about roast beef hoagie orders since the computer (or a ghost using the computer) seems to order them randomly throughout the year. It happens often enough that the kitchen manager always comes out to the main bar and restaurant area to check to see if the order is, indeed, really a customer, or if it's the ghost having an attack of hunger. Tony advises, "No one ever touches the computer to make the order. That's always scary."

Unwanted Visitors

Andee advised me that there were things that happened that often made the ghosts more active—more disturbed. Jason confirmed this as he told me about a sub-basement—a sub-basement he wouldn't want to go down into alone. The employees advised that when plumbing contractors go down to the sub-basement, things happen frequently at the Mansion House for two to three months following their visits. Apparently, strangers in the bowels of the House stir up the ghosts. Andee reminded me, "Like Zack said, Tuesday night a vase went flying off the table and landed four feet away! And one night, when we used to have a yellow vase on the side station, it just jumped off the table!"

I wondered if Jeremy was agitated, but was advised that there were other spirits present and that they were certain that they were not Jeremy.

Andee continued, "One night, I was coming up the steps alone at about eleven o'clock—it was a Friday night. I was picking up the vacuum cleaner and going up the steps. And…there was a woman singing behind me. She was singing 'la la la la la.' I turned around to look to see who was there because the voice was clear as a bell. There was no one there. There's no radio down there. No way for that voice to be behind me." She stopped her story and looked at me with wide and knowing eyes. "Then at the top of the steps, I remembered—duh…stupid…it's a ghost." I laughed.

Andee believes, but is not absolutely certain, that the lady she heard was a cooking wench from a time past. It's just a feeling she has. But the feeling related to the cook is not her only strange feeling. There is something dark downstairs as well. A dark shadow that has the feeling of a death related to the Underground Railroad that ran through the area. She looked uncomfortable and said, "I'm sure it's just a feeling..." But the hair on the back of my neck was standing. And I knew that it was more than a feeling, though she wanted to believe otherwise.

One More Time, for Old Time's Sake

Before I left, late that evening, I could not resist the urge to go into the now darkened dining area to see Table Two again. The rose was at rest now, no movement in the quiet and low light. Andee walked past me from behind and called out, "He's stopped now. It's been still for quite a while." And she continued on to the kitchen.

Tilting my head as I looked at the rose in the dim surroundings, I whispered out loud, "You can turn for me if you want—actually I'd like you to do that for me." Seconds ticked by in my brain as I was sure that the rose incident was some air issue that I'd not identified. There was no doubt in my mind that the air was still now. The quiet told me that. Suddenly, as I was thinking that what I'd seen earlier was somehow a fluke, the rose began to turn. I was shocked. I moved closer to the table. I reached out. The rose still turned.

And then I did what I didn't think I'd have the courage to do. I picked up the vase with the turning rose, thinking that this movement would surely stop the rose's busy agenda of turning and turning.

But that didn't happen. The rose continued its journey around and around as I held the vase in my hand. I just stared, and then, finally, set it back on the table. It turned a few more times and then stopped.

"Thank you," I whispered. The rose turned once again—a full circle—and then stopped.

"Good night, Jeremy…" I said to no one. Or someone.

My advice to you? Ask for Table Two.

The Phoenixville Public Library

183 Second Avenue
Phoenixville, PA 19460
Phone: (610) 933-3013

Anyone who has seen the first *Ghostbusters* movie is familiar with haunted libraries. After all, no matter how modern a facility, one can get the creeps walking down empty isles of books stacked from floor to ceiling—even if the book volumes are neatly positioned and filed in complete alphabetic or numeric order as they are in the Phoenixville Library. But try it once. It's quiet. Listen to the silence. Then picture the haunted librarian from the movie—I believe Dan Ackroyd called her a free-floating, full-torso, vaporous apparition.

Of course, when you have a ghost in a library—or anywhere for that matter—history is the first clue to the who, what, when, where, and why of the haunting. Phoenixville Public Library at Second and Main is no stranger to history. A beautiful historic building dating from 1902 (through the charity of humanitarian Andrew Carnegie) not only has a rich history that gives reverence to the written word, but also has an exciting and interesting sidebar. It's haunted.

Executive Director John Kelly advises that the library was actually started in 1843 by businessmen who felt that the community needed to have a viable resource for family, business people, school children, and others for accessing literary works. They started what was called a subscription library (library services restricted to members only) and called it the Phoenixville Library Company. From that, in 1857, the Young Men's Literary Union became involved, making 500 books from Reverend Jennison's (pastor of the First Presbyterian Church) collection available for library usage. Initially, they were located on the corner of Main and Bridge Streets. "We don't know for sure," says John Kelly, "but the Phoenixville Library Company and the Young Men's Literary Union merged, because somewhere after 1843-1845, there is no mention the Phoenixville Library Company. The library, as it was, bounced around from location to location until 1896, when the state legislature made it a law that school districts could own and operate public libraries. After the law was passed, the Phoenixville School District and the Young Men's Literary Union must have gotten together because, around 1899-1900, the community for the school district got the idea to request money to build a library from Andrew Carnegie. So, in 1902, after much discussion in the community, the Phoenixville Public Library was built at the corner of 2nd and Main."

From the time line (which, by the way, is available in detail through the Phoenixville Historical Society in their publication, *1902-2002 Carnegie Building, Celebration of a Century*), it's safe to say that the current ghosts hail mostly from 1902 forward.

The first mention of ghostly presences came very early on—in the mid- to late 1900s. But it wasn't until the 1940s, '50s, and '60s that people were willing to admit that there was "something going on" at the library. And it wasn't until the 1990s that people with clairvoyant abilities or a sixth sense from areas outside Phoenixville felt comfortable enough to step forward to tell the stories out loud. Prior to that time, community and library staff people would talk about feeling things—an odd shiver up the spine in certain areas, a knowing that something was watching or just outside peripheral vision, hair standing up on the back of the neck. Nowadays, people involved with the library talk about more than a cold chill—they are seeing things, too!

There have been so many incidents of late, that John didn't know where to begin. "I didn't necessarily believe it when I first came here, but since I've come to work in the library these last ten years, I've seen a book jump off the shelf and felt wind coming up my back as I come through the security gate. There's also a person on staff who refuses to go into the attic or by the computer area because she has that feeling of someone being there. That someone is a man—middle aged with a beard. He's supposed to have a dog of some kind. We don't know the name, but more than one person has had that feeling. Something is there." John

Kelly is a definite believer, as he's had the experience of interacting with these silent entities roaming the isles of books.

Flying Books and Strangers

One notable incident began as John was standing at his office doorway looking out over the lines of book shelves in the library. He was very still, in deep thought as he was preparing in his mind for an important presentation that he would be delivering soon. As he stood there thinking, he saw a book pop off a shelf and fall to the floor at the end of one of the  isles immediately before him. At first he thought little of it, as he moved forward, scooped up the book, and read the title—*101 Careers.* (With a laugh, John mentioned that he hoped it wasn't a sign of some sort!) Quickly, he moved around the isle to look into the next isles. His thinking was that maybe someone was on the other side, and that person pushed the book, making it come zipping through. There on the adjoining isle stood a scruffy man with a long beard holding two bags—a strange old man. "Is this yours?" John said to the man. "The man just smiled at me—a very nice man he seemed—and shook his head *no*. He didn't speak at all." John turned and went back around the isle to replace the book on the shelf. He told me that, sometimes, if a book is sticking part way out or the bookends are loose, it might be possible for a book to fall.

But this wasn't the case for this book. The bookends were tight. So tight that it was difficult to even squeeze the book back into it's rightful place. "It didn't slip out," remarked John. "And all the books were evenly placed. There is a backing to this shelf—no way for someone to push a book from the other side. This whole incident took about five seconds." John, seeing how closely packed the books were, quickly stepped back around the isle to question the old man again. But he was gone. Disappeared.

John went immediately to the circulation desk, which is nearly in sight of the area in question. He felt that no one could leave the area without being exposed to the staff members at the front checkout area. This day, someone was manning the desk, as John came to ask if anyone had seen the old man. "There's no one like that in the library," said the staffer. John was not convinced. It was strange, to be sure, but the man had to be in the library. Because if not...

He searched the library; and that took him no longer than a moment or two. He wanted to believe that he'd just missed the man as he left. But that wasn't the case. No one saw the man leave. "It was then that I wondered whether I'd seen an apparition. There was no way he could've gotten out of the library and down the steps in that amount of time—he was too old."

Whistling, Wind, and Little Girl Haunts

And this was not the only time John was exposed to a library ghost. Early one morning, prior to opening, John came in to get some work done in the quiet and still of the day. As he unlocked the door and came in to walk up the steps, he heard friendly whistling. Looking around, he wondered if his mind were playing tricks on him. But he reminded himself that a mind doesn't play tricks as often as things happen at the Phoenixville Library! It was possible that someone was outside at the book bin, returning books or waiting for someone. But when he checked, no one was there. He heard the whistling again. It was inside the building...and he was alone. Could it be the little girl that haunts the children's area in the basement, the playful spirit that staffers have come to know?

Twice now, South Jersey Ghost Research has come to investigate the ghosts at the Phoenixville Library. When one of teams was examining the available paranormal data in the Carnegie Room of the library, an investigator felt as though a little girl was following him. They traced the girl downstairs into the Children's Library. John noted that the library was possibly located along the route of the Underground Railroad, and that people were being rushed to safety through this very area. This, of course, is just conjecture, but it has been considered a possibility that the little girl and her family—or possibly just the girl and her mother—were coming through the Railroad channels, and the mother and child were somehow separated. Possibly the little girl lingered on the very corner where the library was built many years later waiting for a mother who could never come back for her. "We don't know what happened to this little girl," said John, "but she ended up staying here. And 200-250 years ago, we don't know if anything was built on this corner or not. We do know that 105 years ago there was nothing on this corner."

Further research, through the Historical Society of Phoenixville, tells us that, as far as was recorded, nothing stood on that corner 200-250 years ago, and that it was most likely farm land. It is believed that the actual Underground Railroad did not have passage through this part of Phoenixville, so if the young girl wandered in the area, there was probably another explanation for her being there. Having said that, no one knows for sure how passage for the Underground Railroad was obtained in all cases. Regardless of the child's reason for residence, she's there at the library—and making herself known!

Security for Ghosts

As we began to tour the library so that I might see some of the places where occurrences had been wide-ranging over the years, we talked about the prior two research studies completed by South Jersey Ghost Research. I was particularly intrigued by the arched security gate that stands at the upstairs entrance to the main library area. This is a gate that not only keeps people from

One of the library security gates—this particular gate is located in the Children's Library.

accidentally taking unauthorized material out of the library (I always picture red flashing lights and bull horns advising that "You have be caught!" when I see these machines), but it is also a counter. It counts people as they come and go. And it's very easy to hear the machine count. One walks through the arches and the machine registers: Click, click. Two quick little clicks for each person walking through. Click, click. Easy to hear, easy to understand. Click, click. The machine provides a beam that goes across the archway. When the beam is broken, the machine counts the person walking through who has disturbed the beam with a click, click. Simple. Beam broken, click, click. Beam not broken, no click, click. Even I—engineering impaired—understood.

I walked through the machine—and I didn't have unauthorized material, so there were no bells and whistles—just a quick click, click counting me. He had me walk back through again. Click, click. I got it.

This is where John alerted me to an interesting phenomena. Once he'd explained the internal workings of the machine, he asked me to carefully listen as he walked through the arches. He walked through. I heard click, click. Then, I quickly heard another click, click as though someone had followed him through the arches. The beam was broken again just after he walked through.

"Hmmmm," I said, wondering if I'd heard correctly. "Do it again," I suggested. Again he walked through the arches. Click, click and he was through. Immediately after, click, click. I had John walking back and forth several more times. Then I went through several times. Each with the same results. There was an invisible entity breaking the beam as it followed John through the arches. But not when I went through.

"When the Jersey group researched the library with very impressive equipment for detecting high intensity radio waves that depicted things other than normal sounds—plus digital cameras and all that kind of thing—I was going through the security arch and I asked if their equipment was doing something to our magnetic security gates," said John, remembering clearly the strangeness of the episode. "Every time I went through the gate, two seconds later there was another clicking noise, as if someone was following me." The team advised that they felt that this, indeed, was a ghost. Possibly, because John was the curator of the library, the energy there was respecting him and following him to make sure that he was keeping things in order. It wanted him to succeed and to continue to have a place to dwell. I was quick to note that this felt absolutely true; and there was no doubt in my mind that the beam of the security gate was being broken by something following John Kelly.

John, also, is a believer of this follower. "The units are seventeen or eighteen years old," he says, "but I don't understand why the beam is interrupted if no one is there. It either works or it doesn't. And it only counts when the beam is broken. That's how it works. So if the beam is there, it seems to me that the beam wouldn't be broken or another number clicking over, unless someone is following me through."

John told me that the high tech equipment brought by the Jersey team went "off" every time John went in front of it. Not picking up voices or movements, it showed readings consistently around John, even though it should not have been showing this kind of disturbance near anyone. No one else caused the machine to show readings of this nature. He was assured by the team that the equipment they were using was working properly, and that they felt that the energy was absolutely following him around.

"So I began to believe that maybe I do have something here. Maybe there is some energy following me around. But I don't feel it. I mean if it's there, that's fine. As long as it doesn't hurt me." I nodded whole-heartedly, as I eyed the machine suspiciously.

You probably know my thinking, after the rose incident. I whispered near the machine, "You can follow me through—just once—to show me you're real and actually here...." I walked through the machine. Click, click. I pouted. "Just once?" I asked. I walked through again. Click, click, pause, click, click. "Thank you," I said. Now I was absolutely sure. Haunted.

John told me that, on another early morning, he went through the gate and a cold wind came around him, blowing his hair from the back. He went quickly to check the two windows to see if someone had left them open. They were closed and locked. "Then where is the wind coming from," he'd thought. The air conditioning was off that time of the morning—it was the job of the first person in to turn it on for the day. "I'm sure it was the ghost making its presence known," he said.

Ghostly Reading and Carnegie Fears

Near the same area of the library where John saw the strange old man, the New Jersey team found yet another ghostly area. During both investigations, this area (only about twenty years old) gave people having a sixth sense a very uncomfortable and dark feeling. Interestingly enough, the books in this area match the darkness of those feeling the darkness. Historical books about war and death, with titles having the words Armageddon, ghost soldiers, Hitler, devils, and such in their titles. I, too, felt a shiver in this area, there to teach those who will listen about a sinister past.

Several employees at the library have felt the presence of spirits over the years, as well. Having occasions to interact with strange feelings, odd occurrences, and ongoing episodes of the world beyond seems to be a prerequisite to working at the Phoenixville Library these days for many employees.

Unfortunately, a valued library associate and friend died recently, leaving the others at the Phoenixville Library both sad and feeling a great loss. This woman's daughter—very sensitive and autistic—has had a sixth sense experience ever since she was about three years of age. She would not go near the computer room area off the library's main space, the Carnegie Room. And to this day, whenever she visits, she stays away from that area. She doesn't get an evil feeling in that place, but rather a notion that someone is agitated that she is nearby and wants her away from the location. "This has been going on for twenty—maybe thirty—years," John advised me as we strolled.

The computer room in question is situated near the old front door of the original building. One of John's former assistants, during closing one evening, was near these doors. As she opened and then closed the door, she felt someone tapping her on the back and heard someone say "Hi" in a soft voice. She was very upset and rechecked the area. Nothing. No one was there who might have touched or spoken to her. She quickly secured the area and left for the night. Later, John spoke with her about the incident. Some small amount of time had passed and she'd convinced herself that it had merely been the sound of the door closing and that no one had touched her. She'd imagined it. It was her choice not to believe.

But knowing the history of incidents, John believes that she really heard and felt something. He pulled the door open and allowed it to swing shut for me. "Does this sound like it could have been a mistaken voice?" he asked me. I was sure that the squeaking sound that the door made as it shut could never be confused with a voice of any kind. One of the ghosts may just have felt friendly—or mischievous—that night.

Ghosts in the Attic

"There's a presence in the attic," John said as he led me into the small front foyer where the friendly ghost of the former

A photograph taken in the library attic by the Chester County Paranormal Research Society showing orb activity.

assistant was perceived to be. He pointed at the door that led upward to the attic. But first, he showed me a bronze plaque on the wall dedicated to a librarian from long ago. John thinks that possibly this well know benefactress of Phoenixville might be one of the ghosts who roam the isles of books in this day and time. The plaque reads: *In loving commemoration of the eighteen years of happy beautiful service of*

Elmira W. Pennypacker as librarian, 1898-1916. Erected by her friends.

John took me, then, through the locked entrance to the old winding stairs up to the attic. "Many people get an eerie feeling when they come to this place," he told me—including him. "In fact, there is one employee who refuses to go into the attic at all. She'd gone there once and came back upset and agitated. Again, not that there is a negative feeling there, but there is definitely a playful entity traveling about the rafters and storage areas." The room was not that different from most attics one sees. This was a place to store Christmas decorations and other items that need to be pulled out from time to time for one reason or another. Very clean and orderly (despite John's apologies of it not being so.) One thing I noticed right away was that there was no dust or grime—thinking that, were this my attic, I believed that it would definitely be more cluttered and grungy.

One of the investigators belonging to South Jersey Ghost Research became physically ill and could not return to the library after visiting the library attic. (This, I've been advised, is how some people react to manifestations and does not indicate a negative or positive spirit—just that there is a spirit of some kind.) All who feel the entity in the attic, including the Jersey team, say that the spirit there is a playful one. This team took many photographs in the attic and spirit orbs were visible everyplace in their photographs. In this area and also in the main room of the library—the Carnegie Room—there were hundreds of orbs photographed. (See their investigation information at their website: http://www. southjerseyghostresearch.org)

"It's not the dust, either," said John. "There were just too many of these orbs. And if you look hard enough, usually you can see dust particles floating in the air if dust is present. You don't see dust particles in this attic."

I took time here to ask John who he thought was haunting the library attic. "People visiting here and feeling that sixth sense—people who don't know each other—have thought that the person was a younger woman. Perhaps forty to forty-five years of age."

When the Chester County Paranormal Research Society set up a camera in the attic during their second investigation of the library, the camera—hooked securely to the tripod—was ripped from the tripod and thrown down. Whoever is in the attic seems to be camera shy.

Good, Clean Stories

The basement was our next interesting spot! John told me that anyone who has the ability to feel a presence from a supernatural source knows that there is a playful entity in the basement. No one knows who it is, but things have been happening there for a very long time. The people experiencing odd things the most are the cleaning folks.

"Things happen a lot to them," remarked John as he explained how one of the bookends came off the shelf, flew across the floor, and landed at a cleaner's feet. That definitely scared the worker. John noted, "When you see the area, you will see that that is impossible for something like this to happen—unless there was some sort of wind storm in the room." I noticed that there was no source for wind or moving air as we entered the room. "Another thing that happens to one of the other cleaning folks—and this happens a lot—has to do with the plastic trash bags that they have on rolls sticking out of their back pockets as they go about emptying trashcans. A big wad of bags, long," he said gesturing the size to me. "You don't want to go back and forth to get trash bags all night long, so they keep them with them. There are trashcans all over the place! Every once in a while, the bags will start flittering really fast in their back pockets—moving back and forth rapidly. It's not like you can make it happen by normal body movements. Something is making it happen."

I asked, "Does that scare them?" (Thinking that it would definitely scare me.) The cleaner told John, when he'd asked the same question, "No. But, I know it's a ghost because I can't run fast enough to make the bags flutter like that."

The cleaning people also have heard strange noises late at night while they are working. John added, "They've asked me if the library was haunted because they hear things early in the morning or late at night while they are working." Apparently, when they are working downstairs, they hear furniture moving upstairs. It is as if all the furniture is being moved around all at once. They go upstairs, thinking someone is in the building that shouldn't be there at that hour. Checking on the noises, they always find nothing amiss on the upper level. Returning to their downstairs duties, suddenly they will hear it again. But no one is there. And the furniture has not been moved.

And then there's the crash. Both John and the cleaning staff have heard this manifestation. Suddenly, a tremendous crash, as though someone has taken the heaviest thing available upstairs, and then slams it to the floor from a great distance, and with great force—a loud, booming crash. One morning, John heard the sound and, at first, thought it might be the close-by racket caused by a trash truck. But there was no trash truck—nor anyone else around. The area outside the library was deathly still, as was the inside.

I wondered how often such a sound was heard and was advised that it happens often. "You just never know," said John. "You'll be working away and all of a sudden you'll hear a tremendous crash or you'll hear all the furniture moving."

A Child is Watching

The strongest energy area, according to the second South Jersey Research investigation of the library, is located in the Children's Library that· was reconfigured from a storage spot on the lower level in 1920. A staff member with an incredible sixth sense during that investigation recognizes an older women from around the 1890s—probably between sixty and seventy years of age. Another woman has appeared, as well, to her, but is much younger—possibly twenty-something. John thought that the identity of the elderly woman might be the first director of the Phoenixville Public Library—Miss Elmira W. Pennypacker (mentioned earlier on the plaque near the attic). Maybe Elmira floats among the living at the library, keeping watch over those who would carry on the wonderful tradition of books.

John further relayed that the Director of Children and Youth Services at the library was at his desk one night, attempting to get work done, when the spindle pen and pencil holder on his

The Children's Library on the basement level of the library.

desk started spinning around. He jumped back startled and then stopped it with his hand. Five minutes later it started spinning again. So he said out loud, according to John, "Whoever you are, would you please not do this? I'm trying to get some work done, and this is very annoying." But he didn't wait around too long after that, and since the library was closed, he decided that it might be a good time to leave! (I tried to make the holder turn by asking, like I did at the security gates, but the ghost didn't feel like cooperating.)

Thus ended my investigative interview at the public library. I came away thinking about my written report of the odd goings-on at this magnificent building, and thought, what better place to read about ghosts than in a haunted library?

The Investigation

After my interview, there were more developments, however. The Chester County Paranormal Research Society scheduled a formal investigation to take a close look at what was happening at the library. Their findings were exciting and the research seemed to grow legs.

Investigators found several paranormal-like phenomena while there late one evening. There were, of course and as expected, photos of orbs throughout the library. One of the most interesting was translucent, which Investigator Starr advises, according to her theory, that this is "an apparition gathering energy in order to come forth."

But there was an even more exciting piece of evidence—and this one has people around the nation clamoring to the CCPRS website for more information. Investigators Starr and Ritchie actually caught on video a flying book. During their EVP's recordings (see glossary for explanation) the night of the investigation of the newer section of the library (behind the main desk in the left corner), they asked if there was someone there who could move a book, or pick a favorite book in some fashion. They found two books on the floor in the very last aisle that were not there prior. Then they asked, if the books were indeed moved by whoever was there, to please do it again. The video camera was set up at the end of the aisle, and in the footage, the book can be seen coming out of the side aisle, hitting the books along the outside wall, then hitting the ground. The book was thrown with a great deal of force. "Every time I watch it," says Investigator Ritchie, "I get goose bumps." She adds with zeal, "THE FLYING BOOK CAN BE SEEN CLEARLY ON THE VIDEO TAPE!!" Oddly enough, the "favorite" book chosen by the ghost to throw was entitled *Qigong* by Angus Clark. None of us knew what the book's title meant until we looked more closely.

Qigong, according to the Qigong Association of America, is the skill or practice of cultivating energy. In other words, it can be considered movement of an energy force. How appropriate. I do believe the ghost at the library has a good sense of humor!

This was not the first flying book, as those as the library are well-aware. John Kelly notes that this kind of activity is all too common. The news media quickly noted the phenomena, and stories have been flying as fast as books.

But that wasn't the end of the flying book incident. Because of this strange phenomenon, the team was invited back to do another investigation. This time, I was able to participate. This, now being my third investigation, was not as new and strange as it had been before. I was familiar with the procedures—the equipment setup, the mapping of the location, and the varied investigation techniques. Part of the Team Yeti—affectionately called so because of an internal joke about one of the team members who is very tall—we began our part of the rotating investigation in the children's library in the basement of the library.

It was a strange feeling being in the library at night with low or no lighting. I'd been using the Phoenixville library for research, for pleasure, and for take-away fantasies into varied authors' worlds for over two years, and this was a new sensation. For much of the time in the basement area, our group found no evidence of activity, but as we began to relax—letting our recording equipment do the work, we noticed that as Investigators Isaac Davis (of Yeti nature), Cindy Starr-Witman, and I were talking about the paranormal in general, the EMF readings began to rise around Isaac. Sitting comfortably, chatting from a rocking chair with a digital EMF recorder in his lap, the numbers started to rise. It seemed that someone was interested in our conversation. We snapped pictures and kept talking. Soon, the invisible eavesdropper left us alone. This was to happen twice that night.

Later, in the upstairs computer room, Isaac was again the draw for an invisible encounter. The EMF meter numbers rose and, though the photograph was not conclusive of true paranormal activity, it certainly was strange with light streaks that seemed interested in Isaac. Reflection? Possibly. It's still under investigation.

During the exploration, I had only one incident that felt paranormal—and it was quite unexpected. It happened in the attic. When John Kelly had taken me earlier to the attic (during our initial interview), I'd felt nothing, saw nothing, and captured nothing on film. I'd just listened to him talk about all the things that other people had felt and seen there.

This night, I was the second in line going up the twisting stairs to the attic behind Isaac and Cindy. About half way up, I got a sudden jolt of … itchiness. I'm thinking that it's the same feeling that one has when the hair on the body is standing on end. It wasn't a physical response to fear—I'd been here in the attic before with no incident whatsoever. This was something else. I immediately announced it to the team. Then an anxiety hit me. Now, I'm familiar with my own brand of anxiety and this was not that! It was something else entirely. I still did not feel fear, or any kind of anxious feeling, but my heart had sped up (without my consent!) and my breathing became difficult. This lasted for only a short time—the time it took for me to ascend from the middle of the staircase to the top. Then it disappeared. Minutes later, had I not announced the impression to the team, I'd have questioned whether I'd felt it at all. (An important practice is to declare all suspicions and sensations out loud to the team at the time of occurrence and on the recorder for further investigation.) There were no other paranormal episodes for me there.

Later, when our team was in the nonfiction book section, there were strange shadows (this was the location of the flying book), but we could not tell if the shadows were from a natural cause (i.e., the windows) or some other strange source.

The one thing still under investigation is

Chester County Paranormal Research Society Investigator Isaac Davis in the library computer room, located off the Carnegie Room.

a strange voice that came over all the walkie-talkies. The entire group heard a whispering voice say, "Left to right." No one understood the meaning. Everyone thought that someone in the group was talking to someone else about camera equipment setup. But no one could identify the voice—we just all know that it did not belong to any of us.

The most interesting and—probably for me—the thing making me the most uneasy was the shadow. In the nonfiction area of the library, in the same location involving the flying book, we captured on film a shadow moving into the camera's recording lens and then slowly back out. Those of us there saw movement that looked like shadows, but could not identify where the phenomena was originating ... until the film!

I'm afraid that this investigation just brought out more questions about the Phoenixville Public Library! John Kelly advised me that an employee talking to people at the Phoenixville Senior Center was not surprised at the phenomena. It seems the seniors say that they've been hearing stories since the 1920s and '30s about the library.

It would seem that hauntings at the library are "old hat" for much of Phoenixville. It might do well for you to remember that if you happen to take out a book!

(For those of you who would like to hear the EVPs and see the videos of the investigation, it should be available at the Chester County Paranormal Research Society website at http://www. chestercountyprs.com/.)

The Fountain Inn

498 Nutt Road
Phoenixville, PA 19460
610-933-3021

It doesn't seem difficult to find inns and taverns in Phoenixville that are haunted. Because Phoenixville was the site for revolutionary war activity, Underground Railroad passage, and had an important ironworks, it's only natural to have a few ghosts about. Each ghost seems to be surrounded by historic presence. Thus is the case for the Fountain Inn. Writer Meg Daly Twadell tells in her article, "Inns, Tales, and Taverns of Chester County," of horrendous hardship due to the British invasion in 1777. The people of Phoenixville were heartily harassed.

Bees for Your Trouble

One tale that warms the heart, however, and makes one wonder about the ghost in the basement of the Fountain Inn, begins with beehives. It seems that a local beehive farmer, upon seeing the British tramping towards his farm, had his wife and son take his beehives to the Fountain Inn, where it was assumed they would be safe. They were guardedly invited in through a back window, and helped in the hiding of the beehives in the tavern room. It was unfortunate that they were seen, however, and the British were unkind to those dwelling at the Inn. Destruction of the Inn followed as soldiers tore through it in a rampage. When General Cornwallis made his way to the house, he stopped the pillaging, but had his soldiers continue a search to see if there were arms against the crown hidden away. Cornwallis found the people at the Inn to be guilty of harboring arms against the Crown.

Unfortunately for the General, the search of the tavern room was not a pleasant nor positive event. Pulling white sheets off the beehives upset the thousands of bees residing in the hives. A vision of bees attacking British soldiers may have been quite amusing to Phoenixville folks at the time.

But, is it a soldier from this incident or another that has people seeing the unidentified ghost of a soldier cowering in the corner of the basement of the Fountain Inn? A stone marker just outside the front door of the Inn tells visitors that this is as far as the British were able to reach in the British invasion of the northern colonies during the Revolutionary War, September 21, 1777.

Dennis, the current Tavern Manager for the Inn, wasn't sure whether the soldier was from the Revolutionary War or the Civil War, but the people who actually saw the fellow have all felt very strongly about what they saw. A soldier lingers at the Fountain Inn.

Night Watchers

And, of course, the Inn also has its share of other strange happenings. Dennis told me that he knew that the people who lived atop the Inn have seen ghosts, but personally, he'd not seen one. He had, however, felt their eerie presence one night, when he was alone, closing up the tavern. It's normal practice to check the building to make sure that there are no straggling customers still enjoying the early morning hours. He found that there was no one in the kitchen and the bathrooms were empty, as was the beer room.

Working there for a long time, Dennis is able to quickly identify the sounds of the building. He could recognize footsteps of the people living upstairs, and tell which doors opened or shut by their sounds. This one particular night, he heard the lady's bathroom door open. Someone unauthorized was in the building. "I didn't know what to do right away," he said. "So I went in the kitchen and grabbed a knife. I walked around the whole building looking for something—somebody. Nothing was there. The bathroom door in question was shut—but I did feel a strange presence. I didn't see anything, but the hair on my neck stood up." He relaxed after that because he'd been told that the ghosts at the Fountain Inn were friendly. "They don't normally come into the bar area," he continued, "because this area has been changed so many times. There have been people, though, who have seen—late at night—a ghost standing at the fireplace."

The Colonial Theatre

225 Bridge Street
Phoenixville, PA 19460
610-917-1228

The Blob Festival

A book about the paranormal and strange things would not be complete without considering one of Phoenixville's premier events held every summer for seven summers running on Bridge Street: The Blob Festival. This fun and quirky event celebrates the wonderful "B" movie—one of the greatest—The Blob, filmed in 1957 (with scenes in Phoenixville taped in 1958) and staring the late Steve McQueen (his very first starring role in the movies).

The historic Colonial Theatre stars right alongside McQueen in the movie as the giant menacing silicone monster terrorizes the townsfolk while they sit watching the Colonial's screen in the movie. Even a few residents from Phoenixville were used as extras in the film; and "The Blob House" (as affectionately called by locals) at 3rd and Main Streets was used in the movie as well. Now, every summer, the town re-enacts the famous running-from-the-Theater-screaming-in-horror scene (called the Running-Out Reenactment), allowing Phoenixville residents the chance to experience the excitement of the original moment.

Initially named the Colonial Opera House, the Theatre was built in 1903. Used in the beginning as a vaudeville house, the Theatre brought live entertainment to a quiet town. But who knew that a movie such as this would create such a stir in the world of science fiction and for the town of Phoenixville?

The blob itself has become quite the star for this town. Originally, it was made as clear silicone, but after filming began by Valley Forge Films of Chester Springs, blood-red dye was added to make it even more menacing and horrible. Two gallons of silicone was all it took to make the effect real, using miniature sets of the locations involved in the town turmoil. The red dye was truly terrifying to movie fans because this film was one of the first made in color. People were not used to seeing blood-red monsters on the movie screen.

The movie has a typical 1950s theme—man against nature (rather man against a very nasty, blood-red, terrifying nature). Steve McQueen played a teenager in the film—a good guy in a time when teens were not usually portrayed as good guys—who tries to save the town from a monster that munches townspeople for its diet. Of course, few believe the warnings, and more and more people (we all know now that these people are Phoenixville people) are eaten, allowing our monster to get bigger and bigger with each meal. I won't spoil the ending by telling you how our hero saves the town, because if you haven't seen the film, you should.

Fun Times at the BlobFest

In 2005 and 2006, I was lucky enough to witness the wonderful Running-Out Reenactment. It was a hoot, and something that no true lover of the strange and paranormal should miss if near enough to Phoenixville to participate. Of course, there's the opportunity to acquire Blob souvenirs, see the actual fire truck used in the movie (in the 2005 festival), get your picture taken with the Blob, and any number of other fun things. People dress up in scary costumes and 1950 era clothing to celebrate a time of fantasy that indeed can take one away from the troubles of the world.

Beginning the weekend, a blood-curdling Scream Contest chooses the best screamer to open the next day's events with a shriek to end all shrieks. Live music, a street faire, costume contest, parade, and showings of The Blob are all a part of the festivities.

Story Time with the Blob

For me, the Blobfest was the perfect time to acquire stories of ghosts because, as I mentioned, people interested in the paranormal try not to miss the Blobfest if it can be helped.

As a new member of the Chester County Paranormal Research Society, I was invited to talk with people about their ghost encounters as we introduced the idea of ghost research to the community. Here are a few of the Blob day stories collected from attendees!

The Eagle Tavern
Route 100 in Eagle just outside Phoenixville
Phone: 610-458-5331

Brenda Eastham told her ghostly account of visiting the Eagle Tavern for dinner one evening. At one point, she needed to use the restroom. Going to the second story where the bathrooms were located, she went inside, finding that she was alone as she let herself into one of the two available stalls. She did not hear the outside door open indicating that another customer was entering, but suddenly she had the feeling that she was no longer alone. Looking under to the stall next to her, beneath the enclosure, she could see black old-fashioned shoes. The shoes were not from this time. Quickly she found her way out of the restroom!

Around the Foundry and Pennsylvania House Apartments
Jason Melder used to live in the Pennsylvania House on the north side of Phoenixville. Though he's not had a paranormal experience there specifically, he does remember cutting through a field between there and the foundry area as a shortcut to his job site.

Near this field is an old tin-type tower that looks like a brown smokestack and an old abandoned house. He says, "Going by there, I would have goose bumps and feel a horrible fear. I sense that something very bad happened there." For a long time, he felt that he was imagining this feeling of intense anxiety, but realized that now he has a sixth sense about these feelings—not that it doesn't scare him to know that he can seem to pinpoint areas of unsettled happenings. He's gone back to investigate, to actually see if he can find out what has him spooked about certain places. "I just know when harm was done. It causes me to have anxiety attacks. Very weird stuff," he said.

I'd say so. The Foundry has a long history going back to 1875, and though Jason was only on an outlying area of the building, he was sure something was not right.

A Valley Forge House

An anonymous storyteller told a chilling tale of a home that is very close to Valley Forge near Route 23. The family living there would hear continual knocking on a door, only to find that no one was at the door. This continued until they finally closed off the door in question. But the knocking didn't stop just because the door was no longer used. In fact, the knocking has been persistent for over thirty years—and continues today.

Fort Washington Park

Jill Sprague, who is no stranger to the paranormal after a negative Ouija Board incident in New Jersey, has felt an unusual energy at Fort Washington Park in Phoenixville. "There's a trail that runs along the woods, and you know that you are being watched when you walk there." She told me that as she walks along, an unknown presence seems to be peering out from the woods, always watching. "And the weirdest thing is that there is a cemetery, as well, with headstones that tell of 'X' amount of people dying there. Apparently a big battle of some kind took place there and many people were buried in one place." An eerie place.

A Spring City House

Kimberly Jones had a very interesting ghost story to tell me, occurring just outside Phoenixville in Spring City. She was living on the second floor in an old Victorian house that had been broken into apartments. Occasionally, she would hear a baby crying. One particular day, a friend was in the kitchen cooking and when she came into the room, he said, "Were you talking to me in a baby voice?" She was not, having been on the other side of the apartment at the time. Kim tells me that others have heard the baby, as well.

Interestingly enough, one day the landlord came to fix a bad leak occurring in the ceiling above the toilet. When the ceiling caved in, behind the rubble was a blue and a pink parasol. "The room used to be a nursery," she told me.

"It doesn't scare me at all," advises Kimberly. "Whatever it is in the apartment, it's good. It's not like I get a bad vibe or anything."

She told me that her neighbor below may have also seen a ghost. One day the woman woke to find another woman standing in the doorway of her bedroom. There was no one there.

Kimberly has an 1873 map showing the home but she believes that it's much older than that. When the roof fell, they'd found that the house had been insulated with hay. According to her mother, the building used to be a boarding house and then later turned into apartments.

Penn Hurst in Spring City

Kimberly Jones also had a eerie story about Penn Hurst in Spring City, a building that used to be a mental institution in the early 1900s. One day, she and a friend were unlucky enough to be inside the building when they heard a basketball bouncing and bouncing. They went up to the second floor to investigate and found many basketballs on the floor—all flat. There would have been no real bouncing that day.

The Grim Reaper

Another local story talks of a local Phoenixville man taking care of his ill father at his home. Early one evening, while he was sitting with his father, he noticed a figure outside of the bedroom window. He got up and went over to look out the window and saw a figure standing there as if waiting for something. He described it as being a very tall figure dressed in all black with a black hood. He had chills going down his back and returned to his father's bedside. The man's father passed away during the night, and the man swears it was the Grim Reaper he saw, coming to collect his father's soul.

LaTaverna

1193 Valley Forge Road
Phoenixville, PA 19460
610-935-2778

I first heard about LaTaverna from Sheila Cain-Coghill. She advised me that at one time the establishment had been known as Bull Tavern and was a frequent resting and meeting spot for Lafayette and Washington during wartimes. It was said that there were often elaborate parties held there. "Lafayette and Washington are said to have advised their officers that their parties were not at all appropriate. They reminded them that they could barely clothe and feed their army. They should not be throwing these lavish parties."

Visiting the popular tavern and Italian restaurant, I had the opportunity to speak with Jennifer Knapp, a waitress there and also a follower of the Wiccan religion. This particular religion believes in worshiping the mother earth, mind mediation, and bettering yourself and the world around you. The religious beliefs have given her a greater understanding of the world and a comfort level with spiritual things—like ghosts.

Her particular experience at the LaTaverna involves not herself, but another bartender at the restaurant. Downstairs, beneath the bar area, is where the large beer coolers are located, used to stock the upstairs bar. The bartender went downstairs and saw who she thought, at first, was her boss right behind her on the stairs. But it was not. Instead, a dark figure was there, lurking close. And then it disappeared.

The figure is about them so much, though, that the bartenders are quite accustomed to going in and out of the cooler area—the shadow figure doesn't bother them. Jennifer says, "But when I go down there it's just dark and creepy, and you can feel that there is something else there."

The Seven Stars Inn

Route 23 and Hoffecker Road
Phoenixville, PA 19460
610-495-5205

Jennifer Knapp is also a waitress for the acclaimed Seven Stars Inn and she advises that there is quite a bit of ghost activity there. Most of the activity is up on the third floor—they serve on the first three floors and the fourth is an attic, according to Jennifer. She was working one day, and she saw a coworker go up the stairs to the third floor. Having a question to ask her, Jennifer followed the young woman up, talking to her all the while. The coworker went into a room where the bar was located—and disappeared. It was not a coworker, though from the back, her appearance would indicate so. It was a ghost!

Jennifer says, "I thought she was just walking away from me and not hearing me—and all of a sudden there was nothing there. But I definitely saw a figured woman. I think this place has a couple different kinds of spirits."

Others have had stories to tell, as well. Jennifer says, "Someone has mentioned seeing a gentleman behind the bar upstairs. A couple people have seen the same woman that I've seen—dressed somewhat like a waitress. The waitress uniforms are white collared t-shirts and then a kind of v-neck dress with thick black straps on the shoulders coming down into a long dress below the kneecaps. And that's exactly what hers looked like. Except you couldn't see any of the white—just mainly a black figure. I swear I even saw her ponytail. A lot of waitresses won't even go up to the third floor without somebody else going with them."

Still another person advised me that her daughter's boyfriend saw someone coming from the attic. He was quite shaken about it and refused to tell anyone what he saw until after his mother showed him the book, *Ghosts of Chester County,* that described that there were indeed ghosts at the Seven Stars Inn.

The Shadow Valley Ghost Hunters advise that there are several ghosts that have been sighted on the Inn's grounds. "The spirit of a young boy has been seen in an upstairs dinning room (formerly a guest room of the inn). The spirit of a middle age man has been seen on several occasions, always looking down the second floor stairwell. He is believed to be a former owner who, in his old age, had fallen to his death in this stairwell while supervising the cleaning ladies. The most prominent spirit is that of a woman who had hung herself in the third floor attic." (Could this be the woman that Jennifer saw?)

The Manor House

210 Virginia Avenue
Phoenixville PA 19460
610-983-9867

Innkeepers Chaim & Harriet Chachkes of the elegant Manor House Bed and Breakfast Inn will tell you that though they have never personally experienced any paranormal activity, eleven guests who say they are psychic have experienced ghostly activity while there.

My first visit to this wonderful bed and breakfast was very relaxing. Not only were Harriet and Chaim the perfect hosts, but also the house itself held warmth that permeated to my very soul. Harriet told me that the first time a guest reported a ghost incident for this eighty-year-old home, the attic was the area of manifestation. A large number of small, happy children were felt there. At first, she tended to dismiss the report, not being a real believer of ghosts; but then a second, third, and fourth person reiterated the same phenomena. And these were people who did not know one another.

Author and ghost expert Charles Adams came to visit the Chachkes and felt the presence of a boy sitting on the stairs as a large ghostly dog circled--they seemed to be waiting for someone to come home.

It seemed that every person who felt activity in the home, reported small children. Harriet and Chaim's research, though, found that there were only three owners and none had small children. But then one day, Harriet received a call from someone who advised her that there had been yet another family living there at one time—the McNabbs. And the McNabbs had eight children. The children, however, were all still living. Charles Adams advised the Chachkes that it was his feeling that people can leave their electricity behind—in other words, you don't have to die in a place to leave a residual energy.

Another incident at the Manor House involved one of their guests in a rather friendly but insistent fashion. A woman staying the night came down into the kitchen the next morning and said to Harriet, "It's not you! I was awakened this morning by a red-haired, curly-headed woman shaking the bottom of my bed." Indeed, it was not Harriet. It was very interesting that someone else informed her that Mrs. McNabb had curly red hair.

Some time later, the McNabbs actually visited their old homestead and were very accepting of the stories. They felt that the red-haired woman was their mother's sister, who had a very electric personality—if anyone were going to leave a ghostly field, it would have been her. When Harriet inquired about the dog, she was told that there was indeed a deceased sixty-pound dog that fit the story perfectly.

South Jersey Ghost Research came to research the Manor House in 2003 and found extensive activity at the house. They reported not only the residual energy that Charles Adams experienced, but also feelings of being touched and other impressions (see their report on their website: http://www.southjerseyghostresearch.org.) One thing that interested me, upon reading the report that was left with the Chachkes, was that everyone on the Jersey team felt a wonderful sense of well being and calmness in the living room area of the house. I'd not recognized that feeling until I read it in their report. With the little psychic awareness that I have, I know that I felt incredibly comfortable, relaxed, and ready to tell Harriet my entire life story in that living room. It was out of character for me to behave so in a research session. The interview went well beyond what a professional interview should be—and I stayed much longer than I needed to!

Harriet was relaxed, as well, as she told me the stories of the Manor House. "Only one person so far has been truly afraid—she left. She was going to stay three days and only stayed half a night."

This may be the perfect vacation spot!

The Corner Stores

843 and 847 Valley Forge Road
Phoenixville, PA 19460

The Black-eyed Susan Shop
847 Valley Forge Road
Phoenixville, PA 19460
610-917-9965

Kari Katz, daughter of the owner of the buildings at the Corner Stores, has had more than one experience related to paranormal activity at this busy location. Though her grandmother spoke of the history surrounding the buildings to her, the first time she was exposed to it first hand was in 1986. Waking from a fitful sleep in a room above the shop, Kari found that there was a man standing over her bed wearing overalls and chewing on a haystack straw. She knew immediately the figure was a ghost and not a person because she could see right through him. "He was just standing there staring at me. I was terrified. I pulled the covers up over my head and reached over to turn on the light to make him go away. Ever since then, I have slept with the lights on and the stereo playing."

Kari thought that the man she saw was the prior owner of the property. Her grandmother told her that he used to own the buildings. She would often look up to see the owner's wife looking down from the window above what is now a consignment shop.

These ghosts were not terribly old as many of the Phoenixville and Valley Forge ghosts go, though. Kari estimates that the couple owned the property in the early 1960s. The Corner Stores has always housed retail establishments, and the prior owners were probably the only people who actually lived on the property for any length of time.

But then the ghosts became even more interesting. Not long after Kari began to see the spirits of the Corner Stores, she began to hear the clip-clop of horse hooves outside the building. But she could not see an indication of horses, and this was not an area conducive to such traffic. Her grandmother advised that in the 1700s a blacksmith's shop sat on the site. They would repair wagon wheels and shoe the horses. So now, ghost horses have been heard at the Corner Stores.

Lights, Action, Shadows!

Another incident in the upstairs apartment brought footsteps into Kari's life, only without the sound. "I was in my upstairs apartment and the light was on in my living room—I told you I slept with the lights on. You could see the light spilling onto the floor from the living room into my bedroom. Suddenly, a person's shadow—like someone walking between the light and a solid object when you see the light going away and then coming back—crosses by the door. There's no sound (like foot falls) so you know there's no real person out there. So then I avoided having that kind of light source, and that keeps me from seeing anything at all. I didn't like that. The hairs go up on the back of your neck and you can feel it." She shuddered.

Kari laughed a bit then. "Whenever I tell any of my friends about these things, they look at me like I'm crazy. But they have to be here at night when it's quiet. You can't make excuses about doors opening and shutting, or footsteps walking along the floor when there is clearly no one there. You know the sound of creaking floors. You know when someone is upstairs." And something apparently was—a ghost.

The most recent ghost incident happened in 2006 when Kari's parents were vacationing and she was left to fend for herself at the apartment above the shops. "I heard creaking and walking upstairs," she said. "I heard a door shut, and, of course, I know that no one is supposed to be here and that everything is supposed to be locked up. I searched the whole area, looking all over the place for someone. There was not a person there. This happened twice."

Blanketing the Area with Ghosts

One of the scariest things that happened to Kari at the Corner Stores location was the episode of the floating blanket. "I was lying on my bed, and a blanket-like-quilt came down to cover me. I was frozen, watching the blanket. And I'm blinking my eyes and thinking, 'What is this? Am I actually seeing this?' It would float down, then rise back up." I wondered what such a quilt might look like and Kari described something not solid like a real blanket, but like an image of a quilt that you could see though. "I was just terrified; my heart was beating so fast; I was frozen," she said.

Looking at the incident later, Kari feels that the blanket may have been symbolic, having to do with the giving of energy. Researching for herself, she found that this has happened to others.

Preston Dennett, acclaimed paranormal expert and author of *California Ghosts* and *Supernatural California* says, "I have to say, I haven't heard of a translucent-blanket ghostly story before, but I do know that people see ghostly objects all the time, not just ghostly people. They can see ghostly buildings, cars, and furniture, so why not a blanket? I'm just speculating, but I wonder if it was the ghost of someone who used to live there. Maybe that person would use such a blanket or quilt to put a child to bed and covered them with the blanket?" Other speculations may include the ideas that someone was covering Kari with protection or was showing a loving gesture to her personally.

Kari's mother and owner of the buildings, Anne Flaccus, has not had specific experiences like her daughter, but she has mentioned that the television on the third floor has turned on for no reason. She chooses, however, to dismiss this as a power surge.

Kari also mentions, as several other people from other locations, that she sees shadows. "That happens frequently enough," she says. "Shadows, when no one is there. In this house."

Turnaround Café at Corner Stores
847 Valley Forge Road
Phoenixville, PA 19460
610-935-1251

Anne Schimpf from the Turnaround Café, another of the Corner Stores located at the rear of the Black-Eyed Susan Shop, has seen shadows on more than one occasion. "It's just like someone walking by the kitchen door—but no one is there. Or I'll be back in the kitchen area and see someone out in the dining room, but no one is there. This building is almost 300 years old, there has to be something," says Anne. "I wouldn't want to be here at night."

Kari laughed. "They wouldn't do anything to you."

Anne was not so sure. "To you, anyway," she said.

Walking around the outside of the property, Kari pointed towards the Friends Meeting House at the rear of their property, there for about twenty years longer than the Corner Stores, she advised. "There's a cemetery back there—haven't heard stories, but if my dog ran away, there would be no way I was going to go there. I just get an awful feeling. I've walked up there a couple times—you just feel something."

Charlestown Cemetery

Charlestown Road (opposite the Playschool)
Charlestown Township

The Charlestown Cemetery located on Charlestown Road across from Playschool is the most significant Revolutionary War historic site in the area according to the Charlestown Historical Society. Many preservation works have been acted upon over the years, including consideration for eroding lettering and brittle marble. Additionally, Boy Scouts from Troop #67 have had plans to clear away debris, rebuild a section of the wall, clean up the gravestones, and, according to the Historical Society, possibly excavate a tombstone found outside the grounds of the cemetery.

A sheet of tempered glass on a wooden frame protects the gravestone slab of Dr. Samuel Kennedy in this spooky cemetery. Dr. Kennedy was involved closely with General Washington at Valley Forge and responsible for donating the land in Yellow Springs for the first hospital for revolutionary soldiers. In fact, Washington deeply valued his services.

Oddly enough, though no specific details prevail, Dennis from the Fountain Inn was told that there's more going on at this cemetery than most people know about. Acquaintances of his went through the cemetery one night. They didn't touch anything; but when they came out, they were all scratched up! "Supposedly," he advised, "there was some kind of massacre or something like that nearby—there are a lot of soldiers buried there."

Visiting the cemetery myself, with my photographer husband, Carroll Roseberry, we found the area to be disturbing. Overgrown and cast with shadows, the gravestones were beacons for troubled hauntings. Possibly the obituary record from the Presbyterian Church Cemetery, Charlestown, Chester County, Pennsylvania, for Samuel Kennedy (according to www.ushistory.org) is strangely appropriate—even after all these years. Who then can identify the just?

In memory of Doctor Samuel Kennedy,
Physician of the General Hospital who departed this life on the
17th day of June 1778 — 48 years.
In him the patient friend
Harmonious here till death his life did end,
The Church's pupil and the State his care,
A Physician skilful and a Whig sincere,
Beneath this tomb sleeps his precious dust
Till the last trump reanimates the just.

Having heard this particular short story third hand, the impact of its strangeness to me was somewhat limited. Even so, it was a ghost story of the area and I was planning to include it in the book. Part of that process, then, was to get the appropriate creepy photograph that would accompany the story.

The cemetery, situated deeply within a forested area, could be dark even on the brightest of days. Going at the end of my workday to take photographs, which seemed to be the only available time to me of late, would have put me at the cemetery near dusk. Once the time came to secure the photograph, I was having second thoughts about shrugging off the horror of the story I'd been told. I began thinking that I was planning to go there at the same time that those in my story had visited—thus being all scratched up upon leaving the cemetery. I'd seen and experienced many things since the beginning of my research for this book, and decided that the best course of action (just to be on the safe side) was to take photos on a Saturday morning—and not at dusk when the ghostly inhabitants seemed to prowl the grounds.

So, Saturday morning came and it began hot— humity touching me even in the shade of the tall trees in the cemetery. Immediately before going inside the walled area to visit the tombs of the past, I pulled the reading glasses (that I always wore sitting atop my head for convenience) down to read my camera settings. All was fine. Letting myself inside the cemetery through the rusty, wrought iron and gated opening in the stone walls, I looked about the area. The grounds were overgrown with weeds and many varieties of grass and groundcover. The tombstones were old, most unreadable, and of many varied sizes—like crooked and poorly cared for teeth from the mouth of a sleeping monster. At some, though, small American flags were at the gravesites, held in the ground by little stick-like poles. People still cared.

I was not really "creeped out," as I'd believed possible before coming. I'd reminded myself that this was a third-hand story. (Someone told Dennis, who told me.) And it was a bright and shiny Saturday morning. Not dusk. No storms or lightning. No howling winds.

Snap, snap. I took all the photographs I needed, without mishap. Or so I thought.

Upon leaving the cemetery, I sat on the edge of my car seat with my legs outside the vehicle. I didn't expect to find scratches on my body, but I did expect to find ticks from all the greenery. (Everyone hates ticks.) Again, I pulled my glasses from atop my head to look at my jeans and shoes.

The lens on the right frame of my glasses was cracked. Not a big crack. And since my glasses were the plastic variety, the crack just resembled a nasty scratch that makes the world one peers out to a bit blurry in one particular spot. But it was a crack nonetheless—a crack that had not been there when I'd gone inside the cemetery walls.

Nothing had touched me inside the walls. No branches, no flying objects. I'd not dropped my glasses. There was no reason at all that these glasses should have been damaged. But they were.

I looked back to the cemetery beyond my car, at the shadowed gravestones standing jagged in the resting place of heroes and others unknown. I gulped. ...Lesson learned about doubting the stories I'm told.

The Forge Theatre

241-243 First Avenue
Phoenixville, Pennsylvania 19460
610-935-1920

It's been said by the local townsfolk that the historic Forge Theatre is haunted—and quite creepy at night. It seems that prior to being a Theater, it was a funeral home. The Green Room, where actors and actresses check in to stage their performances, was once used by a mortician—it was an embalming room.

In fact, the owners of the prior funeral home, Neiman and Sons, have been fondly remembered by those at the Theatre—they've named their ghost Mr. Neiman. The presence felt at the Forge Theatre is a male ghost, and he has been seen hovering around the costume loft and the stairs leading there, which are frequent places for paranormal activity. Oddly enough, the elevator that went, in prior times, up to the embalming area does not seem to be haunted. Even more curious is that the stairwell to the costume loft, which was merely a storage area for the funeral home, is quite haunted.

But regardless, people have been known to be wary at times alone in the Theatre. One staffer told a story about the uneasiness performers have toward the place. She'd not had particular incidents occur in her presence but knew that episodes had happened to others. It was snowing very badly outside one evening, and she thought that she might not be able to get home after the show. She'd brought a sleeping bag and the things she needed to spend the night. Those about her were disturbed. "You're not really planning to spend the night here?" they'd asked. She hadn't had to stay after all and felt that she'd been quite lucky.

Another tale has been heard about the basement of the Forge. One young lady has seen what she terms "poltergeist activity" there. A poltergeist actually threw books at her! Also, she says, "The toilets occasionally flush themselves—the handles actually move." She thinks that basically, though, the ghosts at the Forge are benign.

The message on their website says: "Our Box Office and Men's Dressing Room are located in the elevator shaft that was once used to transport bodies from floor to floor (but we did finally get around to filling in a suspicious drain in the Green Room floor). The ghosts of the past mingle with our plans for the future. When we're lucky, they help implement those plans."

Charlestown Road (near Stables Bar)

Phoenixville, PA

A lovely three-acre homestead on Charlestown Road near the Stables Bar in Phoenixville is quite haunted. Chris and Lisa Gazzillo should know—they lived through it. It all began innocently enough. When they were young, they began playing with the infamous Ouija Board. As kids do (I know this from personal experience!), they blame one another for pushing the planchette. But, of course, no one was pushing it. No one was making it spell out the letters—D I E—to the young girls. The young ladies were not amused, however, at the abuse the board was offering and they decided to destroy the board. They stabbed it.

That may have been a mistake.

Shortly after the destruction of the board, weird things began to happen in their house. It's possible that they'd invited a bad spirit into their teenage world.

They began to hear someone running up and down the basement steps when no one else was in the house. They'd hear conversations—people talking who weren't there. Chris was very disturbed by the occurrences, "My younger sister and I used to be awakened in the middle of the night, being held down in our beds. We would literally feel hands holding our arms and legs down and pushing our heads backward. We couldn't move. And there would be loud screeching in our ears. It was awful."

Talking about the house, Lisa and Chris had a theory that the house may have been built on Indian burial grounds. "That land had been vacant for a long time and had been swamp land back in the day," said Chris. "Someone else had tried to build on it, and their house collapsed. My father and his father built this house."

The Woman in White and the Boy Without a Mouth

Lisa had further stories to tell. Their brother, Andrew, was about seven or eight years old at the time of the incident—a time, advised Lisa, when children are still seeing spirits. At about three o'clock in the morning, he would see a blonde-haired woman in white, appearing at the edge of his bed, sitting there in a long flowing white dress. She would be crying. At first, he would think that the woman was his mother, who had much the same appearance. He would reach out to her saying, "Mom, Mom..." But this woman was not his mother. Rather it was a foreign woman, one he'd not known or seen before. This happened almost every night, scaring him so badly that he was found each morning curled into a ball on the floor in his parents' room. For years, he would slink in fear out of his room at night to get away from the apparition and find his way to the floor of a safer room.

But that was not the only ghost to terrorize Andrew. There was another ghost boy without a mouth who came to visit. The boy was about the same age as Andrew, and he used to peer out at him through the banister in the stairwell. The banister of the stairwell was right outside Andrew's bedroom, and the little boy would be looking at him through the rails. The boy had no mouth. "He would torment my brother with his presence. He would never try to do anything to him, but he would stare at him and scare him. This is very scary, especially if you're just a seven or eight-year-old boy. And again, Andrew would be found in a hall every morning scared to death on the floor of his parent's room, away from his own room."

Lisa wondered why the boy had no mouth, but there is only conjecture. Was there child abuse, or was his tongue cut out for some horrible reason, or his mouth bound? No one knows.

But these two recurring ghosts brought terror to the household and particularly to their younger brother.

Both Lisa and Chris were amazed at the brazen behavior their ghosts manifested. "We'd actually see stuff," said Lisa. "They'd do stuff right in front of us. We'd be talking and the windows would be closed, but the curtains would be swaying back and forth. You just felt when they were there. Watching you."

One night, their younger sister woke to find a boy sitting on her bed. She thought it was their brother and was angry that he would not allow her to go back to sleep. He kept talking to her. She told him to go back to his own room, but he wouldn't stop talking and he wouldn't leave. So, eventually, she just ignored him. The next morning, she confronted her brother about the incident. He told her that he'd not been in her room that night. It was the ghosts again.

Demons in Phoenixville

Chris was witness and participant in a very chilling episode when she was about twenty-six years old. She'd been sleeping in bed one night and suddenly woke, smelling sulphur all around her. Looking up, she saw three demons standing next to her bed. "This was the most horrendous experience of my life," she said seriously. "I turned my light on and they were just standing there."

I wondered what they looked like.

She cringed. "There were three of them standing in a triangle formation—one in front and then two right behind the first, very close together. They looked like walking corpses, with heavy eyes and torn flesh on their faces. They were sticking their tongues out in a lascivious fashion and hissing at me. I grabbed my rosary beads that I kept on my nightstand, and I just yelled over and over, 'I rebuke you in the name of Jesus Christ; get out of my house.' There was a cord, then, that was very much like the material that my rosary beads were made of, suddenly wrapped around them, pulling tightly against them. They were struggling against it. And then, they just vanished," she said snapping her fingers, "like that. I got really scared after that and wrapped the rosary beads around my wrist for protection for about seven years when I slept. I still keep the beads by my bed."

Lisa say, "It can be a little hard to live with sometimes. I'll spread sea salt to do a spiritual cleansing…and follow those kinds of practices to ward off evil. We always have our rosaries. There are definitely tools to keep evil at bay."

Chris added, "Now my sister will tell me when she sees something in my room, and I tell her that I don't want to hear about it. It's been years, and you just get used to it. And if you don't get used to it, you can just go crazy with it. You can't get rid of it. If I feel like somebody's watching me, somebody is."

Some of the other issues happening at the house include noises and shapes. "They will make noises," said Chris. "They'll definitely let you know they are there. We saw a shape of a person in one of the bedrooms just kinda moseying around. And things come up missing and then turn up." There have also been a lot of plumbing problems in a home that's not really old enough to experience the kinds of things going wrong that are.

New Kimberton House, More Ghosts

The Gazzillos moved from the house on Charleston Road to a newer house of about twenty years of age on East Beacon in Kimberton (at the edge of Phoenixville). Ghost activity continued in the new house.

One thing that has always amazed Lisa is the strong perceptions of the animals in the Gazzillo home to ghostly activity. Many people believe that animals (and children) have a superior sense of the supernatural, with the ability to see, hear, or feel things that others are not privy to. But the extent of those perceptions is often frightening.

"We used to have a cat on East Beacon Drive in Kimberton," began Lisa. "I was home one day by myself, and the cat was sleeping on the couch. I'd gone over to pet the cat, and then, all of a sudden, his eyes got big as saucers and his head went up—neck stretched—and he's looking over my shoulder, then back at me, then over my shoulder again and back at me. Unexpectedly, he begins a howling meow, looks at me, looks over my shoulder again at something I can't see. Then he scrunches back into himself and jumps off the couch, running for the door—he wanted out."

Still another animal story at this house involved the family dog, Reek. "I was asleep again," said Lisa. "And it was three a.m. in the morning. I think that's the demon's witching hour—as opposed to noon when Christ died on the cross. Anyway, it was about that time and our other sister who was a nursing student—which means all-nighters—was still awake after just getting home. We have a beagle, and he usually sleeps in the room with her. I'm in the room across the hall from my sister. All of a sudden, Reek just woke up—don't know why—walked to my room, and sat in the doorway. My sister followed her to see what she was doing. The question was, why would the dog wake in the middle of the night with nothing to wake her up? And why just sit in my doorway? The dog was looking up in the air over my head, and her head was moving back and forth like she was watching a tennis match—as if something was floating above my bed, as if something was watching me. Reek is very much my protector. I know its not good when Reek sleeps in my room. That one night, she watched back and forth at whatever was hovering over my body. My sister got scared and began to pray. And finally Reek came away from the room—but she would not leave until it did.

The other family dog, Boobala, will go into the garage and just stare up into the rafters. "We always call the rafter area the beams—the garage has open beams. There could've been flooring there at one time, I don't know for sure. My father has put up plank wood. Boobala is always looking up at the rafters, all the time. He'll get excited and start whining and jumping up as if trying to beg for the attention of someone up there. Every time he goes into the garage this happens. There's nothing there that we see, but again, animals have a different perception than we do.

And animals are not the only ones aware of ghostly activity in the Beacon Drive house. Lisa says, "I can feel when something is not right and when something is in the house. I become unnerved—I always know when they're there."

Another sister in the family found ectoplasm on the walls in the hallway and the walls in the bedroom. "Each one of us has had a time to be home alone," continued Lisa. "When we're home alone, they like to play with us. We'll hear walking upstairs. One thing particularly, they must have used to reside in my parents bedroom, because they like to shut the door and lock it—when there's nobody in there. Then we have to go and get the key, because the door locks from the inside. Sometimes we'll hear the blinds rustling. It can be a little frightening at times."

The Cat Man of Phoenixville and Valley Forge—Urban Legend or Ghostly?

Other things have scared the folks of Phoenixville through the years. Is it urban legend or is there really a "Cat Man?" One young woman told me the following disturbing story about an estate connected to Valley Forge on the other side of the park from Phoenixville. Apparently, if one goes through Chesterbrook and into Mill Creek Park, then proceeds across the street, a paved path goes around the corporate center. As youngsters, they would follow the path down the hill and off to the right—this is where the last remaining ruin of the estate sits, now just a wall.

The tale goes (in her words):

This is the story of the old Urban Legend about the "Cat Man" that lived at the deserted Cassatt Estate (at least I think artist Mary Cassatt lived there for awhile) that was behind Green Valley Stables—all of which became Chesterbrook. I remember riding our ponies through there as kids and scaring ourselves witless with tales of the "Cat Man" that lived in the old deserted servant quarters of the estate. The story went that he wanted to be a cat, and so he grew his fingers long and ate only tinned cat food. The only thing he couldn't do was grow a tail, and so he was very jealous of the cats. Therefore, when he would catch a cat, he would rip its tail off!

The creepy thing was, most of the cats at Green Valley were Manx cats! [Cats without tails.] We kept our horses at Skyline farm, but when I was at Green Valley, I do remember seeing tailless cats. Anyway, we used to really feed into the legend by looking up in the trees, and any scraps of clothing or anything up on a branch, we were sure it belonged to the "Cat Man." I even remember that one time we got off the horses and peeked into one of the abandoned buildings. We saw lots of old opened cans (which we were sure were cat food cans). As you can imagine, to us, that was more "proof" that the legend was true! We used to really creep ourselves out riding through there, imagining we could feel him looking at us and such, until they began building Chesterbrook when I was about sixteen or seventeen.

Quickie Ghost Stories of Phoenixville

The Wawa Ghost

Rt. 113 and Township Line Road
Phoenixville, PA 19460

The Wawa, a premier retail convenience store, is no stranger to supernatural happenings! Oddly enough, though relatively new, always bright and cheery, and filled with customers throughout the day and night, a ghost has been known to roam the isles by the coolers at the Wawa. One night, when two employees were working and there were no customers in the store, one of them heard someone having a conversation by the coolers. The female employee turned to the other employee working with her. Both had raised eyebrows. She said to the male employee, "Were you talking to me?"

"No," was the reply from the male, his brow furrowed.

"Did you hear that?" she asked, goose flesh rising on her arms.

"Yeah, but we're not going to tell anyone, are we?"

"No," she replied, "We are NOT!"

But she told me. And I'll be listening now as I buy my milk.

The Moon Saloon

400 Bridge Street
Phoenixville, PA
610-933-7666

Pamela Barnes, the new owner of the 1894 building now known as The Moon Saloon, has only been open for business a short time. But even so, the ghosts are making themselves known to her.

With an interesting history related to times of true cowboys, this fun and whimsical saloon and restaurant has a ghost or two attracted to bells! In times past, some taverns serving beer were equipped with troughs of running water that allowed drinking male customers to conveniently relieve themselves of body fluids right there at the bar into the troughs. This practice, of course, was not conducive to having ladies present. Therefore, this particular tavern had bell buzzers installed in varied areas of the building. Pamela believes that there must have been a separate entrance for women, and when a lady wished to enter the tavern area, she rang the bell for service. The men would then know that a lady would be visiting and that "things" should be put into acceptable order.

Today the bells can still be heard at the Moon Saloon. But now, instead of the ladies ringing them, ghosts do. Additionally, Pamela adds, "Interestingly, right after I took over this place, at 2:15 in the morning, after everyone was gone, there was a strange couple sitting at the bar. I kept telling them that they had to leave. But they kept sitting there smoking. They acted as if I wasn't there—like they couldn't see me. It was the bells, I think, that called them out."

"Then you think that the people at the bar were ghosts..." I suggested.

She sighed and didn't say anything for a moment. "Like I said, it was strange and they didn't leave." Apparently, suddenly they were just gone.

The Intersection at High and Main Streets

"There used to be a cemetery," ghost enthusiast Sheila Cain-Coghill says. "If you were to go straight down Main Street past the Foundry building across the bridge (called the Low Bridge), the road goes up to High Street. Main Street sort of dead-ends at High Street. Well, that intersection used to be a cemetery back in days of the settlers. And so there are ghosts still there. There have been weird things mentioned around that intersection, and it's always been somewhat a depressed area. I've had a couple residents tell me stories about the Hotel Pennsylvania—which is right there. Lights going on and off after they turn the lights off—that kind of thing. There used to be a marker on the north end, on the river side where some poor guy died in a horrific accident at this intersection, and he's been seen. He was hung up on a gantry or something, and was actually hung. It was an accident. When he's seen, he's up in the air. That's creepy."

The Blue Bonnet Farm

Andee of the Mansion House advised me of a private home in Phoenixville called the Blue Bonnet Farm, a very old stone residence. Knowing someone who used to live there, she heard some very chilling war stories. At the time that her friend lived at the farm, there was a hot tub at the back of the property. While in the tub, one could oftentimes see Civil War soldiers coming out of the woods. The soldiers would disappear right before they got to the hot tub. I believe that would cool the water very quickly!

Park Avenue

Another haunted house Andee of the Mansion House has been privy to was a L-shaped farmhouse on Park Avenue. Her best friend was continually plagued by the silly antics of her ghostly resident. She'd have locked the house tight—latching all doors and windows. Suddenly, all the windows and doors would just pop open. Additionally, her smoke alarms and burglar alarms would go off for no reason. Two things that really made the human residents feel strange were the two big mounds outside the house that the dogs were always digging at—the mounds looked like graves and nothing would grow on them.

Andee's personal involvement came one day when she visited her friend. Cars were in the drive, leading her to believe that they were home and inside the house. She knocked and knocked on the door. Presently, she heard what sounded like cowboy boots walking across the hardwood floor on the second level of the house. The boots didn't concern her because there were horses on the property, and boots were the shoe of the day. There was no answer after about twenty minutes of knocking and calling out.

"I went home thinking she was mad at me for something and didn't want to see me," she said. "But when I called, my friend told me that no one had been home—she'd been out with her mother in *her* car." No one was home, that is, except the ghostly cowboy.

Death Hill

Dayton Street
Phoenixville, PA 19460

According to www.shadowlands.net, on Dayton Street at the top of the hill, a graveyard sits. Tales say that, late at night, ghosts leave their graves and switch places. It is also said that if you stand nearby to watch, the ghosts will come for you. Then you will be put into the grave! Hmmm. Sounds like a tale for the campfire!

This tale could be the remnant of a ghostly story grave robbers would manufacture and disseminate to keep people away from cemeteries and in doors at night while they did their odious and illegal work, providing fresh cadavers for medical schools' anatomy classes. Stories of haunted bridges and roadways were also often sown in communities across the country by the local grave robbers—also known as "resurrectionists"—so upright citizens would not stumble across these men at work in the watches of the night.

Wolfgang's Book Store

237 bridge street
Phoenixville, PA 19460
610-410-5039

Wolfgang's Book Store is located in a strange old building along Bridge Street, and is situated on the second floor. Making one's way to the second floor can be unnerving, however, because the stairwell is so creepy. Not creepy in the way of an old, dilapidated building—because this is clearly not the case—but creepy because the stairs, beyond the second floor, go on and on and on, back into the recesses of the building. Not merely up, but back. It feels as though there are staircases with no end in this building—the perfect place for a ghost to linger, in my way of thinking.

Paul Oliver spoke with me on the evening I visited and related that there had been, indeed, some strange goings on at the shop.

"We were painting and this was our first time here. I was in the bathroom, and I was painting. The door was open and there was a fan for out-take. Suddenly, I heard a voice calling me, and I thought it was my mother, who was here helping me paint. I came out and asked, 'What's up?" She replied, 'Nothing'." She'd not called to her son.

"But I distinctly heard a very loud voice," he said with a serious tone. "A female voice. Loud and very clear."

Ghostly painter or eerie reader? Could this also be the same ghost responsible for the orbs Paul caught on film?

501 Rossiter

Phoenixville, PA 19460

Popular Phoenix News columnist, Connie Bretz, has written about a ghost or two in her column, "Time Capsule." In 2003, she investigated 501 Rossiter Avenue (listed at that time as 501 Valley Forge Road). Connie told me that she spoke with realtor Susie Parr and history buff Peter Brown about "the ghost in the attic." Some people think that George Washington slept there and that his blood was in the attic. Connie advised in her column that, whatever the rumors were about this story, a 1949 clip from the Daily Republican stated:

> The story is that Washington, while at Valley Forge, stopped at the home to drink from the pump in the front yard, which since has been covered over.

The story left me wondering about the blood aspect...

Columbia Hotel

148 Bridge Street
Phoenixville, PA 19460
Phone: 610-983-0300

The elegant Columbia Hotel was built in 1892. Those I spoke with at the hotel and bar/restaurant were hesitant to say too much about the ghosts that roam the building. But roam they do. One employee talked about closing one evening after everyone had left the building for the night. She could hear a whispered conversation in the hallway—one that should not have been there. She asked another employee, "Did you hear that?" When they checked for the owners of the hushed conversation, there was no one there.

The employee advised that there were those who saw and heard things upstairs, and another waiter saw a ghostly woman in the hall that scared him. She herself often felt strange during storms—especially when the elevator would go up and down, its doors opening and shutting although quite empty. One employee I spoke with didn't even want to know about the ghosts—she didn't want to see, hear, or feel them—advising that it would make her feel afraid to be there alone. More details were not forthcoming—there are those who do not wish to speak of presences not clearly seen or identified.

Gay Street

Phoenixville, PA 19460

There are those who have seen a man walking on Gay Street—no one seems to know who he is. He's been seen a lot—but disappears before the looker's eyes.

The Breckenridge Apartments

(Breckenridge Plaza Incorporated)
495 Nutt Road Ste. D204
Phoenixville, PA 19460-3314
(610) 933-4879

Anne Schimpf from the Corner Stores at the Turnaround Café tells a scary story about the Breckenridge apartment complex. "The Breckenridge is haunted. Doors used to slam there for no reason. My aunt's microwave cart had mugs sitting on it, and they just fell—like someone pushed the cart and shattered the mugs. When that happened, it scared us, so we took off running. We came back an hour or so later and all the cups were standing back up on the microwave like nothing had happened. We saw the cups shatter." Anne thinks that a man, at some time in the past, hung himself from the tree that was just outside that apartment on the Nutt Road side of the building near the cemetery. "That's all we really know about the story," she said.

Maybe this ghost was hanging around for coffee...

Yellow Springs Inn

Though not located in Valley Forge or Phoenixville, the Yellow Springs Inn has also been noted as a place to be—if you're a ghost. Rob Lukens, Executive Director of the Historic Yellow Springs, advised that though he, personally, has not been witness to haunted events at the hospital ruins, the Inn (which is right down the hill from the ruins) has had ghostly activity reported. People have reportedly been touched from behind when no one was there as well as other strange happenings.

Found on the property adjoining the Yellow Springs hospital ruins, Dennis (from the Fountain Inn) advised that something paranormal was detected in the basement of the Inn which is now under renovations. A building stood on this site prior to the current inn (pre-1770). Yellow Springs is a wonderful place to visit to check these ghostly occurrences out! (Check out the full details in *Ghost Stories of Chester County and the Brandywine Valley.*)

First Avenue in Phoenixville

Jennifer Knapp use to baby-sit five little boys on First Avenue in Phoenixville. The mother of the children told Jennifer stories of spirit relatives who were there to protect her children. Jennifer says, "You could see shadowy figures coming down the steps sometimes. And you know, being sixteen years old, I would want to check out what I was seeing. The boys were so used to it, it was nothing to them." One of the little boys told her that a spirit shut him in the closet and it wouldn't let him out. He had to bang on the door for someone to hear him. The mother told Jennifer that, right before a car accident, the apparition of a woman appeared in front of her, almost as a warning that her son was about to be hit by a car. "The family believes more in guardian angels than ghosts." She told me, too, that when renovations took place within the house, the ghosts (or guardian angels) became more active.

Reeves Park

Second and Main (across from the Phoenixville Public Library)
Phoenixville, PA 19460

A local resident had this to say about Reeves Park:

...a few years back I delivered newspapers in that area. My paper route went directly past the entrance to the library on the Second Avenue side of Second and Main—I delivered the newspaper to the library itself—at about 3:30 am. One Friday night/Saturday morning I saw, sitting on the bench, a boy and a girl. They were in Victorian-like garb and starring at me in an odd way. Since I only occasionally saw people out at that time of night around Reeves Park, I noted it, but didn't jump to the "ghost" conclusion immediately. Their age, being so young, did concern me but I thought that maybe I misjudged that. How could ten-year-old kids be out at that time of night? During the course of my paper route, I would go around the block and then come back past the library a few minutes later. At that point, they were gone. I didn't see them walking anywhere around town that night, which also seemed strange.

I went home and thought about those two children for a long time. So many of the pieces of this story just have not added up in my mind.

The Hauntings Continue...
Valley Forge National Park

Many stories are told about the starving, ill-laden soldiers at Valley Forge and the ghostly walks that they take at dusk. In 1895 the Philadelphia Press wrote:

> It is said that the spirits of the dead Revolutionary soldiers flit along the hillsides on stormy nights and visit the shadowy spots where they once gathered around the camp fire and that ghostly campfires have been seen flickering among the trees on starless nights and the faint echo of a challenge and countersign could be heard from the lips of spirit sentinels.

This writer also told the stories of the local village people and their homes. One home had been that of a robber. His ghost walked the property after he was shot trying to rob an agent from the railroad station. After the stories and sightings, families of the area could not be persuaded to live in the tenement—even at no cost.

Yellow Springs General Hospital Washington Hall

For Information: Historic Yellow Springs
1685 Art School Road
Chester Springs, PA 19425
610-827-7414

Before going into Valley Forge, then, it may be appropriate to stop by Yellow Springs General Hospital at Washington Hall, America's first military hospital. Constructed in 1778, this was the only hospital that was commissioned by the Continental Congress for the Revolutionary War. It was specifically important to the ill and dying soldiers of Valley Forge. Built on land donated by Samuel Kennedy of the 4th Battalion under Anthony Wayne (see Charlestown Cemetery) the small hospital (by today's standards) was 106 feet long, 36 feet wide, 3 full stories and attic high with 9 foot porches surrounding the first 2 stories on 3 sides, according to the information provided at the remains of the structure. Valley Forge soldiers in dire need filled the hospital before construction of the building was even completed.

From the plaque outside the ruins: "Here the sick and wounded were cared for and new recruits were inoculated against small pox. Medical and surgeons' supplies were distributed to the field from this facility. The hospital was closed in 1781 but continued to serve the city of Yellow Springs in other capacities. Fire destroyed the building in 1902, but it was rebuilt. Fire again destroyed it in 1964. Today, these field stone ruins stand as a witness to the brave continental soldiers whose spirits stand silent guard from the unmarked graves around the hospital site."

Standing in front of the ruins, there was a very unnatural feeling. It was much too quiet for the park-like area in the woods. Sound stopped as my photographer and I walked through the burnt rooms that used to house soldiers from long ago. It was said to us that there were probably more soldiers here than on the fields of Valley Forge, because many ended their lives within these now burnt walls. Maureen, an employee for Historic Yellow Springs at one time, told us that she always felt an eerie coldness around all the local buildings that were part of the Yellow Springs and Valley Forge history. "Nothing to put a finger on..." she said. "But something."

Walking through the ruins was indeed a very uncomfortable undertaking. The grounds around it, though well landscaped and lovely, held an aura of mystery. The hair on the back of the neck becomes energized and gooseflesh erupts as one strolls inside the rock-like rooms. But the most disturbing element I felt while there was that quiet. Absolute quiet. No birds singing or bugs buzzing. The air was still and unmoving. Knowing that unmarked graves surrounded the area brought unbeckoned thoughts to mind—of soldiers never leaving this place alive. There were shadows of the past here that brought cold chills.

Only shadows were reported to me around this particular site—shadows and feelings of despair.

General George Washington's Headquarters in Valley Forge National Park

Carol Starr and Kim Ritchie, investigators of the Chester County Paranormal Society in Pennsylvania, spent time in Valley Forge National Park at General George Washington's Headquarters in June of 2006. Greeted by a costumed guide for the building, they were welcomed in with a briefing of historic facts about the Headquarters Building. The house was built prior to 1776 and the only original parts of the building still remaining were the house itself, the wood floors in the rooms, and the staircase banisters.

Still, despite these few remaining items of history, the guide told the investigators a chilling story. One of the other guides—a male, who, of course, wore a male Revolutionary War uniform—

was changing into his costume one day. As he stood erect to check the feel and appearance of the uniform he wore, he felt hands adjusting the uniform from behind—smoothing the shoulders and pulling down on the bottom of the coat. He turned to thank who he thought was one of the other guides for helping, but found that he was alone in the room.

Investigating the building, by taking photographs and EMF (electromagnetic field—see glossary for explanations) readings, they found the EMF meters to be quiet with no ghost activity at that time. On the second floor, however, Investigator Starr witnessed a quick bright flash of light over Investigator Ritchie's left shoulder. The flash was not a camera shot (as their cameras were at their sides), a lightning strike, or possible through any other visible means that they could see. Nothing, however, was visible in the photographs showing activity.

Another story that has been told with frequency over the years with few details available is that there have been sightings by people walking near General George Washington's headquarters of a man hanging by the neck in the nearby woods.

Valley Forge Memorial Chapel

Valley Forge National Park

Investigators Starr and Richie also visited the Valley Forge Memorial Chapel, which was built as a tribute to George Washington and the American patriots of the Revolution. The first cornerstone of the Chapel was laid in 1903. The following details the EMF readings indicating ghostly activity in and around the Chapel. (See Equipment section for explanation of readings— typically, an energy reading that measures between 3-7 milli-gauss may be of a paranormal origin.)

The Low Down on the Chapel
The Parking Lot—active. EMF readings ranging from 2-5.5
No visible signs of electrical sources responsible for readings

Cannons in Front of the Chapel—active. EMF readings from 2-5
Base of the cannon 0 reading; along the cannon's body, up to 5

Alcove and Hallway Running Next to the Chapel—active. EMF readings steady 3-4 along the hallway to about 6 feet in height.

Bell Tower—active. Sporadic EMF readings.

The Chapel, 4th Pew and Front Pew—active. EMF reading of 4 All other pew readings were 0. Nothing artificial to cause the readings at Pew 4 or Front Pew.

Brass Plaques—active. EMF readings 3-4
Going down the center of the aisle, there were large brass plaques. All registered 0, except the one closest to the front. Readings for this plaque were 3-4.

Bibles—active. EMF readings 4
When the meter was placed on top of the Bible, there was a 0 reading. But when the meter was placed along side of the pages of the book, the readings were consistently 4.

Side of Chapel—active. EMF meter reacted and cool breeze blew could be felt. Then the meter went to 0.

Cemetery in Rear of Chapel—inactive. No EMF readings.

So what do these reports indicate? Answer: There are ghosts at the Washington Memorial Chapel. The ghosts here, though, are most likely of varied natures—not all from a time of war and armies. The Chapel is an active Episcopal parish of the Diocese of Pennsylvania with a full program of worship, study, fellowship, and services. Additionally, it serves as a wayside chapel for visitors to the area. Because of this, many people from many times and places have taken advantage of holy worship in this chapel. And therefore, many different spirits may have been exposed to this peaceful and beautiful resting place.

Fields of Valley Forge

Valley Forge National Park

The fields around the Valley Forge Park are not only beautiful, but they act as a re-enacting place for the ghosts of the past. Many have told tales of soldiers running across the fields and then disappearing into the dusky landscapes. Author Charles Adams shared with Harriet Chachkes of the Manor House that battlefields are the spookiest place for anyone to visit. Even the cynics, he says, become uncomfortable when they are near a battlefield.

Within the fields, huts can be found that depict the living conditions during the Revolutionary War. Some have been built at later times, simply a historic reference; but some of the huts have original parts. Those are the ones that show positive (by orb activity) in photographs and give EMF meter readings showing ghostly presence. One such hut found, after winding through the park along the inner line defenses, displayed a spirit orb just as dusk was turning to dark.

The Waterman's Monument

The Waterman's Monument is a fifty-foot granite obelisk that was erected in 1901 by the Daughters of the Revolution. This is the only site in Valley Forge that has an identified and marked grave. Lieutenant John Waterman from Rhode Island died on April 23, 1778, and was remembered here by this grand structure. Sometimes orbs are clearly seen on photos around the monument, especially at twilight. (Though one of my photos did, indeed, show such an orb, the quality of the photo was not appropriate for this book. But it made me wonder: Could the orb have been the brave Lieutenant, or one of the other fine soldiers that roam these fields or merely a ghostly energy from another realm?)

The General Anthony Wayne Statue

General Wayne was a colorful character during the Revolutionary War. It seems his fiery enthusiasm took him into and out of trouble throughout the war. Some called him quick-tempered and very opinionated, but he was a fighter and earned the name Mad Anthony for his heroic ways.

Born near Philadelphia at Waynesborough in Chester County, Wayne was named after his grandfather. Having held a variety of positions in the Continental Army, he was part of General George Washington's long winter of 1777-78 at Valley Forge.

His lifespan (1745-1796) is well-remembered in history, and his last days (though not at Valley Forge) are recorded by author Rupert S. Holland in *Mad Anthony,*

In November 1796, the general and his staff of officers went aboard the sloop Detroit. All the town and all the garrison were on the wharf to bid him farewell and a mighty chorus of cheers arose as the sloop pushed off and headed south to the lake.

Lake Erie was covered with whitecaps and the sloop made slow progress against head winds and waves that rocked her from bow to stern. The voyage had not continued long when the general began to feel his left leg growing increasingly painful. The leg was swollen, and each lurch of the ship made it ache anew. The discomfort was mounting when the sloop, after a long, stormy voyage, anchored in the bay off Presque Isle, an old fort that had been built by the French, had been held for a time by the British, and was now occupied by a few Americans.

To this fort, with its crumbling walls overgrown with ivy, that watched over the lake from the southern side—where the Pennsylvania city of Erie was afterwards to rise—his aides carried the general, and they tried to make him comfortable in a bed in the main blockhouse. There was no doctor in the fortress, none in the wilderness around the lake. The commander of the post sent a messenger to Philadelphia, another to Fort Lafayette, but both those places were far distant from lonely Presque Isle.

Days passed. Gales lashed the lake and sent the spray flying above the windows of the fort. The last of November brought snow. For two weeks in December, Wayne fought the inflammation in his leg. But with no skilful surgeon at hand, he had to fight alone against that old wound, received so many years ago from the bullet of the sentry outside Lafayette's headquarters on the River James, and against the gout that had followed in the wake of the wound.

Early in the morning of December 15, 1796, the commander of
the post, who was watching by Wayne's bedside, heard the general
murmur: "Bury me at the foot of the flagstaff, boys."

That was the last message of Anthony Wayne. They did as he
asked.

But it's what happens after General Wayne's death that is bizarre and ghostly. Ghost Investigator Carol Starr picks up the story from here. "Moving forward thirteen years to 1809, Wayne's daughter, Margaretta, was quite ill herself (she died the following year and was buried at St. David's) and made a request of her brother, Isaac, to bring their father's remains back to the family burial plot at St. David's in Radnor. No doubt expecting his father's body to be fairly decomposed after thirteen years, Isaac makes the trip in a light wagon. However, things did not turn out quite as planned.

Isaac arrived at Erie and enlisted help from a doctor—and possibly several other people—in exhuming the body of Anthony. Despite the passage of thirteen years, the general's body was nearly perfectly preserved, and it was quite obvious that Isaac's small wagon would not be large enough to carry the body back to eastern Pennsylvania. At this point, the story takes a decidedly odd twist.

It is decided that only the bones would be sent back East with Isaac. This was accomplished by cutting the body of the general into pieces and literally boiling the flesh away from the bones! The question arises as to whether or not Isaac knew about the entire process or was simply presented with the bones after the fact, but it is known that the flesh itself, along with the instruments used, were re-interred in the gravesite by the flagpole in Erie.

Burial number two took place at St. David's in Radnor, Pennsylvania, when Isaac returned, an event attended by a large number of dignitaries of the area.

Considering the entire story, it is certainly easy to see how the legend of General Wayne's ghost grew—that would be one mighty confused spirit, I would think!"

Investigator Starr continued with the ghost tale. "A tour guide at Valley Forge Park shared a story of General Wayne's statue, which is located in the park. On clear nights with a full moon, the head on the statue rotates!"

Still another legend tells us that so many bones were lost along the road during the trip from Erie to Radnor—an area that encompasses much of our modern-day Route 322—that on January 1st (on Wayne's birthday), his ghost can be seen wandering along Route 322 looking for his lost bones.

Beyond the Soldiers at Valley Forge

A Child Walks

There have been those, too, who have seen strange things at Valley Forge that did not align with war or starving, sick soldiers. One such story tells of a child ghost. Hit by a car sometime in the 1950s, the child can be seen walking along the roads around Routes 23 and 252 at dusk looking, perhaps, to continue a journey started so long ago.

A Lantern Beckons

Still another story for travelers along Route 23 is that of a man carrying a lantern. He swings it back and forth as though warning those on the road to slow down—and then disappears. (Could he be a protector of deer?!)

The Valley Forge Beef and Ale

827 S Trooper Rd, Norristown, PA 19403

610-666-1520

A waitress (who wished to remain anonymous) for the Valley Forge Beef and Ale told an unnerving story about a ghost named Fred. One night as she was bartending, she had her first opportunity to experience the paranormal. A customer at the bar was drinking a bit too much, so she decided to drive the lady home for safety purposes. She said to the lady customer, "Whatever you do, do not leave the building. I'm going to go upstairs, take care of my closeout, and then I'm going to drive you home." Suddenly, while upstairs finishing up her work, she heard a horrible scream. She ran downstairs to find out what the screaming was about.

The woman yelled, "There's a demon in here! It went right through me!"

The waitress knew that others at the restaurant had seen a ghost there quite frequently, and that one of the cooks had named him Fred. But she'd not seen Fred.

The lady continued, anxious and scared, "He's an evil ghost! Let's get the h— out of here!"

Trying to calm the customer down, the waitress helped her into her car. She pulled from the driveway and suddenly her car horn started beeping and would not stop. It was as though someone was holding the horn on the steering wheel down, the sound loud and irritating. The customer was screaming for her to stop blowing the horn—but our waitress wasn't blowing the horn. "I yelled right back at her," said the waitress, "I'm not doing it!"

Having time to think about it later, she wasn't sure whether the ghost was following her out to the parking lot and began beeping her horn or if some other coincidental incident had caused the mishap. Still, she feels that this is the only encounter that she, personally, has had with Fred.

The girls that work the day shift see him all the time, she advised me. He wears a black hat. Interestingly, it is believed that there was a murder next door to the tavern back in the 1970s or earlier. Could Fred have something to say about that?

The People Who See

But what about the real people who actually see, feel, or experience paranormal manifestations in one form or another? Is there correlation or connection between the other world and these particular individuals? As I've researched the material for this book and conducted the interviews of those who have seen things from the world beyond, I've found that in most cases, their sightings are not merely hooked to the places I'm investigating. Their experiences seem to infiltrate their daily lives—wherever they go.

It's as though they've opened a door in their minds that allows them to perceive things just outside the "normal" bustling world. If someone sees or hears a ghost at one of the locations you've read about in this book, in most cases that person with the story will have also had other experiences at other locations. I've been told by several people that ghosts hitch rides with their intended "hauntee," and, therefore, can be sensed in varied unorthodox places.

In other words, ghosts can be hooked to a place as we've all been taught to believe; but it also appears that ghosts can attach to a person and travel right along as a companion on the other side—sometimes good; sometimes bad.

It would seem, too, that once a person has had a true paranormal episode, it is more likely that he or she will experience another ... and another ... New experiences are usually made available from outside our realm to these "psychic" folks in any place known to be haunted.

I can only surmise from the research that both these theories are correct.

Kim at the Chamber of Commerce agrees when she says, "Wouldn't surprise me if I brought them with me." She's always felt the touch of the paranormal and feels that she is definitely in touch with that questionable reality just outside one's vision.

Kari Katz from the Corner Stores can attest to having experiences that not only happen away from the original commercial district for Phoenixville—the trading post—but also at her home in Rosemont. When I asked why she thought that ghosts were drawn to her, she answered, "I don't know. Ever since I was little there was something. I know that in my home, I see a woman holding a baby. She was standing over me when I was holding my sleeping son. "

Her daughter has not been spared, either. (Does the sensing of ghosts run in families? I think it may.) When her young daughter was a bit over two years of age, she would stand at the bottom of the steps pointing upward and say, "Workman, workman." But there was no workman there to see. "Workman go down steps," the child would say.

Anne Schimpf from the Corner Stores at the Turnaround Café has a story to tell as well. She not only sees shadows at the Corner Stores but also has felt the fingers of the paranormal at her home of years ago. This was a cottage that was noted as the oldest house in Phoenixville (across from Seacrist by Bridge Street). "I see people and their shadows. My deceased grandmother was always there and rocked the bed when my daughter woke up at night. Sometimes when my daughter started to cry, the bed would start to rock real slow. My daughter would see a face and ask, 'Who is that?' I would tell her that it was just the reflection of the tree outside. But she would tell me, 'No! That face, that looks like Granny.' My husband worked night shift and this only happened in the night when we were alone and my daughter would wake up crying—the bed would rock. It didn't bother me, though. It was very comforting, because I knew who it was."

At her home on Emmett Street in Phoenixville, Anne told me that her child saw a man with red hair staring in the window. There was, additionally, a ghost that lived in her crawl space. "He would move things toward me or tap me on the shoulder when I was there. I would just say, 'Leave me alone [said in a friendly voice].' He would never bother me and he would never come past the doorway." She knew the identity of this ghost. He'd been the victim of an overdose in the building at one time.

Kari Katz, cringed at the story. "But he touched you and moved your things around!"

Anne was persistent, though, in saying that his manner was docile. "He wasn't throwing stuff at me," she said to Kari with a laugh. "It just didn't phase me...And when I smoked in the house, my daughter would say, 'Mom, a light keeps coming in front of the door.' I would say, 'Oh, it's just my cigarette smoke.' But I knew it wasn't because I could feel something behind me and the fan was blowing the other way. So I know the smoke was going the other way. But I couldn't tell her that—she was going to bed."

Anne reiterated that her daughter saw things as well. "There was the guy with the red hair—she can tell me details of things that she shouldn't even know." And the sightings happen outside of her Phoenixville home for her daughter. "We went to Hopewell and we saw a guy just standing there. He was a ghost. I saw it, too." Sensitivity to ghosts does seem to run in families.

How Do You Feel About Ghosts?

Chris Gazillio is a firm believer that ghosts are attracted to people as well as places. "They seem to follow us ever since we dabbled with the Ouija Board. Our ancestors, coming from the old country, all have the second sight. They call it a gift from God. And our Aunt, who is a deeply religious woman, she had the sight. She would see the future. We've always been aware of spirits in our family. Our sister dreams of the dead, frequently. She always knows the difference between the dreams—when the dead are actually visiting her—and her regular dreams. That contact always leaves her physically a little different." She went on to say about their prior residence on Charlestown Road, "We don't know if the family there now has seen anything or not. I think that people can be haunted as well as houses. And I think that we are."

Jill Sprague was first introduced to the paranormal through a bad Ouija Board experience in New Jersey, and has since felt ghostly presences in the Fort Washington area. She says, "I don't believe that ghosts actually follow a person, but after you have a first experience, it opens your mind up to them." She believes that spirits know when a person is more receptive to a manifestation. A spirit recognizes that after a person has had a paranormal incident, that person is more likely to accept another. "The spirit knows that I will be more receptive to it doing something funny," she said, "Like turning on faucets. I have had that happen to me." Then she became very serious. "But I also know that ghosts can attack people." (Jill learned that when a ghost actually knocked her to the ground in New Jersey.)

Kimberly Jones of Spring City had a near-death experience from an illness that she feels spurred her awareness of the world beyond. "I died two years ago, saw a blinding light—ever since, I'm more receptive."

Jason Melder, who felt fear when passing through a field near the Foundry and Pennsylvania House, has also felt the anxiety that comes along with ghost awareness in other places after his first exposure. "If I go into a certain area, I can sense bad things or possibly an accident. I've actually gone back to investigate and it's scared me. It causes me to have anxiety attacks."

Brenda Eastham, who saw ghostly feet at the Eagle Tavern, says that ever since she felt a presence the first time, she has been more aware of spirits. "I think you become more intuitive to what's already there."

Harriet Chachkes of the lovely Manor House believes that there is something to be said about residual energy being left behind by live people. She says, "You do walk into a house and feel it—like when you are house hunting." And she may be right. Is it possible that the good (or bad) feelings you perceive in a place have to do with a psychic awareness of the place? "If you pinpoint or pigeon hole me, I'm not sure that I believe," she says, "but I can't not believe. The one thing I do not doubt is psychic powers." When asked about her possible ghosts, she says, "I'm very pleased that they're here."

Jennifer Knapp, waitress at LaTaverna and the Seven Stars Inn, is no stranger to paranormal activity. In fact, her early experiences may be why she's able to sense ghostly activity today. "When I was younger," she said, "I used to see shadowy figures all the time. I remember, at one point, when I was little, just being frozen—looking at it. And I wanted to get up and go to my parents' room, but I couldn't. I was too scared to move. When it finally went away, I would go into my parents' room, but they always thought it was nightmares." She knew differently even then.

One positive thing is that her experiences in the past have helped her understand the world beyond and not be afraid of it. When asked where she thought the shadows came from, she answered, "Pretty much a soul that died, and for whatever reason, can't move on. Stuck in this reality but a different realm."

Jennifer, too, cautions about the use of Ouija Boards. "I could do it—so could a couple of my friends. The one time, we were using it in my kitchen, and we started asking questions. We found out later that using the Ouija Board is not technically safe because what you're doing is opening a communication hole between you and another realm. And you have to conduct a certain ritual to close that realm when you're through. If you don't do that, the link stays open."

Jennifer described the usage of paranormal senses (including the usage of tarot cards) that summed up much of what everyone else said. "It's pretty much being able to open the doors in your own mind and just letting it flow from there. It's like a body muscle—you have to continually work it, practice, and perfect it."

That, of course, is if you want to experience ghostly activity!

Just Plain Creepy

As I've researched, I've found that many people described strange feelings about places—nothing that they could really identify, but certainly something that made the hair on the backs of their necks stand straight up. Creepy places. Some of these places, I've mentioned in the local stories recorded here; but there are others, as well, that seem just too interesting not to mention. In some cases there is a lack of firm evidence or conclusive research. Still others here have had ghost sightings, but stories of substantial length were not forthcoming. Some places are local, and others may be outside the Phoenixville, Valley Forge, and vicinity blanket (but within driving distance) and may be worth a visit or drive-through. There are tidbits of information for a few of the locations mentioned, but others, I've only the creepy nature of feelings present as described by people I've come into contact with as stories began to develop. Still, I thought you'd like to see the list.

Heading Home To Phoenixville

J. S. Brooks tells of a fleeting glimpse that haunted him on a twilight drive home to Phoenixville. He said, "Pattern recognition is a funny thing. We're born with it bundled in our brains. It helps us see potential trouble lurking in the underbrush or stalking us through a grove of trees … but it can be fooled. When it is, people say their eyes have played tricks on them. That's what I told myself while heading up North Pottstown Pike on a long, winding trip home through the twilight gloom of a cold February evening. And yet, the image caught out of the corner of my eye was so vivid, so detailed, that I still wonder. The sun was setting red in the west, peeking through a gap in low gray clouds threatening snow, casting long shadows in the fading light. Suddenly, off to the right, I caught a glimpse of a figure standing by the road's shoulder. She was young, maybe in her twenties, with long black hair. Something in her stance and expression gave me the impression she was waiting for someone. However, she was not dressed for the weather. She had no hat, coat, or gloves. Instead she wore the sensible skirt and blouse you'd expect to see any young businesswoman wearing on a mild day. Being a father of two, I was concerned. The day had been cold and the temperature was rapidly dropping. I turned my head in her direction, wondering if she needed help. In the split second it took to swing my gaze fully in her direction, she was gone. Behind where I thought I'd seen her standing was a steep hillside rising to a shadowy tree line. There was a footpath leading up the slope. Yet the hill was too steep and too high for her to have climbed it and disappeared into the trees so quickly. She had simply vanished, if she had ever been there at all. I was left to wonder on the long drive home if I had really seen her or if my eyes had been fooled by the strange alchemy of dim light, long shadows, a twist of tree limb, and a grassy hillside. Had pattern recognition gone wrong and manufactured her, an ephemeral mirage, in vivid detail? Or was she a troubled soul haunting the roadside, awaiting a special someone who never came in life, yearning to return home from a journey interrupted? I'll never know. All I can say for sure is, whoever she was or wasn't, she haunted me all the way home."

Church and Main in Phoenixville

Sheila Cain-Coghill tells of a redcoat officer who was buried right at the corner of Church and Main Streets. "When the family died out, they left the family cemetery there, but it was also used as a potter's field. That's why they planted that redcoat there. He is apparently under the sidewalk on the corner at that location. There used to be a plaque there that said he was there. But the plaque is gone now."

Folklore tells us that grave markers prevent spirits of the dead from leaving their bodies and walking abroad. Without his plaque, is Phoenixville's redcoat free to roam?

Morris Cemetery on Route 23

There is cemetery on Route 23 that supposedly holds many bodies that were dug up from other Phoenixville gravesites and moved to the new location. There are questions, though, about this.

St. Peter's Church in Phoenixville

There have been unsubstantiated rumors of a ghost lingering on the grounds of this holy place. And why not? It's a beautiful location!

Jug Hollow on Route 23

There are some old buildings here where George Washington is said to have stored his liquor. Do spirits return for spirits?

Acorn School House

Malvern near Yellow Spring Road

Apparently, one story tells of a rape and murder here, but the details are not forthcoming ... and no more than shivers document the story.

Citco Gas Station

Next to Corner Stores in Phoenixville

I was advised that Citco tore down a very old building, a place where the Underground Railroad may have operated. As they were demolishing, they caught a glimpse of ... something. It's sketchy as to what that *something* was.

The Phoenix Newspaper Building

More than one person has mentioned the old tunnel beneath the old newspaper building as being creepy, but no news has been reported about true ghosts there.

Mill Street

Phoenixville

The last two houses on Mill Street, I'm told, stand upon the location of the original hospital in Phoenixville, built because of the Foundry. Apparently, there is an angry ghost there who has pushed a child down the stairs.

Varnum's and Huntington's Quarters

Valley Forge

There is, supposedly, a camp ground south of Route 23 that displays a creepy headstone marked with the initials "JW." Other unmarked graves are situated nearby.

Valley Forge Graves

Outer Line Drive as it winds downhill from Wayne's Woods

It is believed that the ground has given way to reveal the knee bones of soldiers, buried in a crouched position. (According to the National Park Service, however, it cannot be substantiated that there are graves in the park. It is possible that animal bones are responsible for the stories.)

The Phoenix Iron and Steel Company

Phoenixville

The 115-year-old foundry in Phoenixville is the last remaining trace of the company. Historic renovation will provide the town with a visitor's center and other possible usage. It has been said that ghostly Revolutionary soldiers frequent the misty hours of the morning ...

Vincent Baptist Church Cemetery

Yellow Springs

This cemetery supposedly houses many soldiers. Do their restless souls still long for the freedom they fought so strongly for?

Norristown State Hospital

Norristown

It is said that there are tunnels underground that connect to the buildings of this historic asylum and hospital, and that ghosts of deceased patients roam there.

The Tree

Phoenixville

Don at Big Daddy's in Phoenixville told me about a very creepy 400-year-old sycamore tree located on private park property off Pawlings Road (just before the bridge and small park parking area).

The General Wayne Inn

625 Montgomery Avenue
Merion, PA 19066

This is a 1700s Inn that is filled to the brim with ghostly activity! (Read the story at www.hauntedhouses.com.)

The Colonial Theatre

225 Bridge Street
Phoenixville, PA 19460

Though the Theatre, according to Director Mary Foote, has not had reports of ghosts, there *was* a report given me by a visitor of a creepy area inside its walls. Historically, the Theatre used to be a Vaudeville show house, and I was told that the dressing rooms under the stage were very creepy—tiny, dark, and cramped.

Valley Forge Springs

Valley Forge

Route 23 near Davis Road is the location for what used to be a town, I'm told. Though only a few buildings were there, those structures are now in ruins. Two of the businesses established there at one time were the Slab Tavern and the Spring Bottling Plant. (It was said that the Spring Bottling Plant was bought by Hires, but there is no evidence that root beer was ever made here.) This is a very creepy place.

The White House

Though people live in the white house on Pawlings near the bridge (before crossing the river near Ferry Road), it has been said that the house is very creepy. One person is quoted as saying, "If that place is not haunted, it should be."

Mount Misery

Valley Forge

There is a story that in Valley Forge Park by Route 252 behind Davis Road, William Penn lost his way as he tried to find friends. Because of this distress, the area was named Mount Misery. (The next day, he did indeed find his friends. The area where they were located was named Mount Joy.)

Afterword

I came to you in the beginning with some ghost experience. I leave with much. There are ghosts. Trust me on this.

—D. P. Roseberry

Special Note From D. P. Roseberry

If you have enjoyed reading this book, you might like to enhance your paranormal experience by participating in the new spooky attraction, Ghost Tours of Phoenixville. There guides will take you on a ninety-minute walk highlighting the most haunted borough in Pennsylvania. For more information, visit their website at www.ghosttoursofphoenixville.com

Glossary and Equipment

As I conducted interviews to collect the ghost stories of Phoenixville and Valley Forge, it was interesting to note that most people
immediately asked questions that involved the identification and
investigation process for ghost hunting. They wanted to know:

- How can I tell if there is really a ghost here?
- How will I know if it's a true paranormal phenomena or some-
thing natural?
- Can you tell me what's haunting my property?
- Can I hunt my own ghost? How do I do that?
- What are all those things [equipment] the guys on television
use to hunt ghosts? How do they work? Do you use them?

My answer, at the time of most of my interviews, was, "No,
I'm not a ghost investigator, but I'll see what I can do to find out
what you'd like to know." It was then that I became involved
with the Chester County Paranormal Research Society, the ghost
investigators for Chester County and beyond.

Chester County Paranormal Research Society (CCPRS) is a
non-profit organization that is based out of West Chester, Pennsylvania, co-founded by authors and paranormal experts Mark and
Katharine Sarro. Coupled with scientific methods and experience,
they lead a group of investigators in research studies in attempts
to validate and prove the existence of paranormal activity. It
was this group that taught me the ghostly ropes of paranormal
investigations.

Since most people had questions about the stories and ghosts that haunted them, I decided that this would be a good place to explain the process of a true investigation and relate some of the terminology and equipment used. Though you may not have seen many of these terms in the stories as told here, when scientific functions are applied to the tales for investigation, these terms and equipment items are used.

Note: The following section is provided by the Chester County Paranormal Research Society and appears in training materials for new investigators.

Please visit www.ChesterCountyprs.com for more information.

Terminology Defined

Air Probe Thermometer
A thermometer with an external probe that is capable of taking instant measurements of the air temperature.

Anomalous field
A field that cannot be explained or ruled out by various possibilities, that can be a representation of spirit or paranormal energy present.

Apparition
A transparent form of a human or animal, a spirit.

Artificial field
A field that is caused by electrical outlets, appliances, etc.

Aural Enhancer
A listening device that enhances or amplifies audio signals, i.e., Orbitor Bionic Ear™.

Automatic writing
The act of a spirit guiding a human agent in writing a message that is brought through by the spirit.

Base readings
The readings taken at the start of an investigation and used as a means of comparing other readings taken later during the course of the investigation.

Demonic haunting
A haunting that is caused by an inhuman or subhuman energy or spirit.

Dowsing Rods
A pair of L-shaped rods or a single Y-shaped rod, used to detect the presence of what the person using them is trying to find.

Electro-static generator
A device that electrically charges the air, often used in paranormal investigations/ research as a means to contribute to the materialization of paranormal or spiritual energy.

ELF
Extremely Low Frequency.

ELF Meter/EMF Meter
A device that measures electric and magnetic fields.

EMF
Electro Magnetic Field.

EVP
Electronic Voice Phenomena.

False positive
Something that is being interpreted as paranormal within a picture or video and is, in fact, a natural occurrence or defect of the equipment used.

Gamera™
A 35mm film camera connected with a motion detector that is housed in a weather proof container and takes a picture when movement is detected. Made by Silver Creek Industries.

Geiger Counter
A device that measures gamma and x-ray radiation.

Infra Red
An invisible band of radiation at the lower end of the visible light spectrum. With wavelengths from 750 mm to 1 mm, infrared starts at the end of the microwave spectrum and ends at the beginning of visible light. Infrared transmission typically requires an unobstructed line of sight between transmitter and receiver. Widely used in most audio and video remote controls, infrared transmission is also used for wireless connections between computer devices and a variety of detectors.

Intelligent haunting
A haunting of a spirit or other entity that has the ability to interact with the living and do things that can make its presence known.

Milli-gauss
Unit of measurement noted on EMF meters, measures in 1000th of a gauss and is named for the famous German mathematician, Karl Gauss.

Orbs
Anomalous spherical shapes that appear on video and still photography.

Pendulum
A pointed item that is hung on the end of a string or chain and is used as a means of contacting spirits. An individual will hold the item and let it hang from the fingertips. The individual will ask questions aloud and the pendulum answers by moving.

Poltergeist haunting
A haunting that has two sides, but some kinds of activity in common. Violent outbursts of activity, with doors and windows slamming shut, items being thrown across a room, and things being knocked off of surfaces. Poltergeist hauntings are usually focused around a specific individual who resides or works at the location of the activity reported, and, in some cases, when the person is not present at the location, activity does not occur. A poltergeist haunting may be caused by a human agent or spirit/energy that may be present at the location.

Portal
An opening in the realm of the paranormal that is a gateway between one dimension and the next—a passageway for spirits to come and go through. See also Vortex.

Residual haunting
A haunting that is an imprint of an event or person that plays itself out like a loop until the energy that causes it has burned itself out.

Scrying
The act of eliciting information from spirits with the use of a pendulum.

Table Tipping
A form of spirit communication, the act of a table being used as a form of contact. Individuals will sit around a table and lightly place their fingertips on the edge of the table and elicit contact with a spirit. The spirit will respond by "tipping" or moving the table.

Talking Boards
A board used as a means of communicating with a spirit. Also known as a Quija Board.

Vortex
A place or situation regarded as drawing into its center all that surrounds it.

White Noise
A random noise signal that has the same sound energy level at all frequencies.

Equipment Explanations

In this section, the Chester County Paranormal Research Society looks at the application and benefits of equipment used on investigations with greater detail. The equipment used for an investigation plays a vital role in the ability to collect objective evidence and helps to determine what is and is not paranormal activity. But a key point to be made here is: the investigator is the most important tool on any investigation. With that said, let us now take a look at the main pieces of equipment used during an investigation...

The Geiger Counter

The Geiger counter is a device that measures radiation. A "Geiger counter" usually contains a metal tube with a thin metal wire along its middle. The space in between them is sealed off and filled with a suitable gas and with the wire at about +1000 volts relative to the tube.

An ion or electron penetrating the tube (or an electron knocked out of the wall by X-rays or gamma rays) tears electrons off atoms in the gas. Because of the high positive voltage of the central wire, those electrons are then attracted to it. They gain energy, collide with atoms, and release more electrons, until the process snowballs into an "avalanche," producing an easily detectable pulse of current. With a suitable filling gas, the flow of electricity stops by itself, or else the electrical circuitry can help stop it.

The instrument was called a "counter" because every particle passing it produced an identical pulse, allowing particles to be counted, usually electronically. But the counter does not tell anything about the identity of the energy, except that it must have sufficient energy to penetrate the walls of the counter.

The Geiger counter is used in paranormal research to measure the background radiation at a location. The working theory in this field is that paranormal activity can effect the background radiation. In some cases, it will increase the radiation levels and in other cases it will decrease the levels.

Digital and 35mm Film Cameras

The camera is an imperative piece of equipment that enabled us to gather objective evidence during a case. Some of the best evidence presented from cases of paranormal activity over the years has been provided by photographs taken. If you own your own digital camera or 35mm film camera, you need to be fully aware of what the camera's abilities and limitations are. Digital cameras have been at the center of great debate in the field of paranormal research over the years.

The earlier incarnations of digital cameras were full of inherent problems and notorious for creating "false positive" pictures. A "false positive" picture is a picture that has anomalous elements within the picture that are the result of a camera defect or other natural occurrence. There are many pictures scattered about the Internet that claim to be of true paranormal activity, but in fact they are "false positives." Orbs, defined as anomalous paranormal energy that can show up as balls of light or streaks in still photography or video, are the most controversial pictures of paranormal energy in the field. There are so many theories (good and bad) about the origin of orbs and what they are. Every picture in the CCPRS collection that has an orb—or orbs—is not presented in a way that states that the orb is (or orbs are) absolutely paranormal in nature. I have yet to capture an orb photo that made me feel certain that in fact it is of a paranormal nature.

If you use your own camera, understanding that camera is vital. I encourage all members who own their own cameras to do research on the make and model of the camera and see what other consumers are saying about them. Does the manufacturer give any info regarding possible defects or design flaws with that particular model? Understanding your camera will help to rule out the possibility of interpreting a "false positive" for an authentic picture of paranormal activity.

Video Cameras

The video camera is also a fundamental tool in the investigation as another way for collecting objective evidence that can support the proof of paranormal activity. The video camera can be used in various ways during the investigation. It can be set on a tripod and left in a location where paranormal activity has been reported. It can also be used as a hand-held camera and the investigator will take it with them during their walk through investigation as a means of documenting to hopefully capture anomalous activity on tape. Infrared technology has become a feature on most consumer level video cameras and, depending on the manufacturer, can be called "night shot" or "night alive." What this technology does is allow us to use the camera in zero light. Most cameras with this feature will add a green tint or haze to the camera when it is being used in this mode. A video camera with this ability holds great appeal to the paranormal investigator.

EMF/ELF Meters

EMF=Electro Magnetic Frequency; ELF=Extremely **Low Frequency**

What is an EMF/ELF meter? Good question. The EMF/ELF meter is a meter that measures electric and magnetic fields in an AC or DC current field. It employs in a unit of measurement called a "milli-gauss," named for the famous German mathematician, Karl Gauss. Most meters will measure in a range of 1-5 or 1-10 milli-gauss. EMF meters are used in paranormal research because of the theory that a spirit or paranormal energy can add to the energy field when it is materializing or is present in a location. The theory says that, typically, an energy that measures between 3-7 milli-gauss may be of a paranormal origin. This doesn't mean that an artificial field can't also measure within this range. That is why we take base readings and make maps notating where artificial fields occur. The artificial fields are a direct result of electricity, i.e., wiring, appliances, light switches, electrical outlets, circuit breakers, high voltage power lines, sub-stations, etc.

The Earth emits a naturally occurring magnetic field all around us and has an effect on paranormal activity. Geo-magnetic storm activity can also have a great influence on paranormal activity. For more information on this kind of phenomena visit: www.noaa.sec.com.

There are many different types of EMF meters; each one, although it measures with the same unit of measurement, may react differently. An EMF meter can range anywhere from $12.00 to $1,000.00 or more depending on the quality and features that it has. Most meters are measuring the AC (alternating current, the type of fields created by man-made electricity) fields and some can measure DC (direct current—naturally occurring fields, batteries also fall into the category of DC) fields. The benefit of having a meter that can measure DC fields is that they will automatically filter out the artificial fields created by AC fields and can pick up more naturally occurring electromagnetic fields. Some of the higher-tech EMF meters are so sensitive that they can pick up the fields generated by living beings. The EMF meter was originally designed to measure the earth's magnetic fields and also to measure the fields created by electrical an artificial means.

There have been various studies over the years about the long term effects of individuals living in or near high fields. There has been much controversy as to whether or not long-term exposure to high fields can lead to cancer. It has been proven though that no matter what, long-term exposure to high fields can be harmful to your health.

The ability to locate high fields within a private residence or business is vital to the investigation. We may offer suggestions to the client as to possible solutions for dealing with high fields. The wiring in a home or business can greatly affect the possibility of high fields. If the wiring is old and/or not shielded correctly, it can emit high fields that may affect the ability to correctly notate any anomalous fields that may be present.

Audio Recording Equipment

Audio recording equipment is used for conducting EVP (Electronic Voice Phenomena) research and experiments. What is an EVP? An EVP is a phenomenon where paranormal voices or sounds can be captured with audio recording devices. The theory is that the activity will imprint directly onto the device or tape, but has not been proven to be an absolute fact. The use of an external microphone is essential when conducting EVP experiments with analog recording equipment. The internal microphone on an analog tape recorder can pick up the background noise of the working parts within the tape recorder and can taint the evidence as a whole. Most digital recorders are quiet enough to use the internal microphone, but as a general rule of thumb, we do not use them. An external microphone will be used always. Another theory about EVP research is that an authentic EVP will happen within the range of 250-400hz. This is a lower frequency range and isn't easily heard by the human ear, and the human voice does not emit in this range. EVP is rarely heard at the moment it happens—it is usually revealed during the playback and analysis portion of the investigation.

Thermometers

The use of a thermometer in an investigation goes without saying. This is how we monitor the temperature changes during the course of an investigation. CCPRS is currently using Digital thermometers with remote sensors as a way to set up a perimeter and to note any changes in a stationary location of an investigation. The Air-probe thermometer can take "real time" readings that are instantly accurate. This is the more appropriate thermometer for measuring air temperature and "cold spots" that may be caused by the presence of paranormal phenomena. The IR Non-contact thermometer is the most misused thermometer in the field of paranormal research. CCPRS does not own or use IR Non-contact thermometers for this reason. The IR (infrared) Non-contact thermometer is meant for measuring surface temperatures from a remote location. It shoots an infrared beam out to an object and bounces to the unit and gives the temperature reading. I have seen, first hand, investigators using this thermometer as a way to measure air temperature. NO, this is not correct! Enough said. In an email conversation that I have had with Grant Wilson from TAPS, he has said that, "Any change in temperature that can't be measured with your hand is not worth notating..."

Bibliography

Books

Adams, Charles J., III. *Ghost Stories of Chester County and the Brandywine Valley.* Reading, Pennsylvania: Exeter House Books, 2001.

Grimley, Oliver. *Valley Forge.* Norristown, Pennsylvania: Oliver Grimley, 1952.

Holland, Rupert Sargent. *Mad Anthony, The Story of Anthony Wayne.* New York & London: The Century Company, 1931.

Rowell, Melissa and Amy Lynwander. *Baltimore Harbor Haunts.* Atglen, Pennsylvania: Schiffer Publishing, 2005.

Smith, Kristin. "BlobFest Consumes Bridge Street," *The Phoenix,* July 2002.

Twadell, Meg Daly. "Inns, Tales, and Taverns of Chester County." Publication unknown, n.d.

_____. *1902-2002 Carnegie Building, Celebration of a Century.* Phoenixville, Pennsylvania: Phoenixville Historical Society, n.d.

_____. "A Deserted Village," *Philadelphia Press,* September 8, 1895.

Internet Resource List

www.Ushistory.org
US History

www.phxsg.org
Phoenixville Area Historical Society

www.charlestown.org
Charlestown Historical Society

www.phoenixvillechamber.org
Phoenixville Area Chamber of Commerce

www.nps.gov
National Park Service

www.hauntedhouses.com
Haunted Houses

www.shadowlands.net
Shadowlands

http://southjerseyghostresearch.org
South Jersey Ghost Research

www.valleyforge.org
Valley Forge Convention Center

www.forgeTheatre.org
Forge Theatre

www.thecolonialTheatre.com
The Colonial Theatre

www.yellowsprings.org
Historic Yellow Springs

http://en.wikipedia.org
Wikipedia